S0-BHZ-905

Problems Before Unity

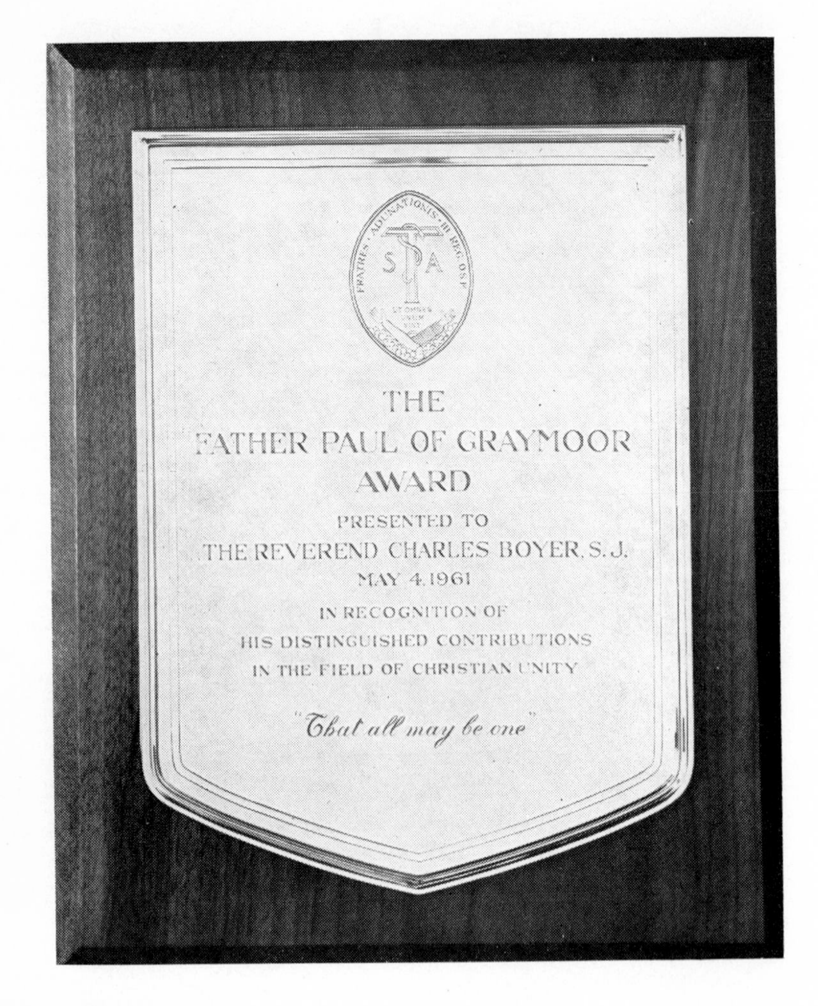
THE
FATHER PAUL OF GRAYMOOR
AWARD
PRESENTED TO
THE REVEREND CHARLES BOYER, S. J.
MAY 4, 1961
IN RECOGNITION OF
HIS DISTINGUISHED CONTRIBUTIONS
IN THE FIELD OF CHRISTIAN UNITY
"That all may be one"

PROBLEMS BEFORE UNITY

Msgr. J.G.M. Willebrands
Shawn G. Sheehan
Paul Mailleux, S.J.
Robert W. Hovda
Walter M. Abbott, S.J.
Gustave Weigel, S.J.
Charles Boyer, S.J.
Bernard Leeming, S.J.
Very Rev. Angelus Delahunt, S.A.

Foreword by Augustine Cardinal Bea

HELICON PRESS Baltimore - Dublin

Helicon Press, Inc.
1120 N. Calvert St.
Baltimore 2, Maryland

Helicon Ltd.
53 Capel Street
Dublin, Ireland

Library of Congress Catalog Card Number 62-18781

This volume consists of the papers presented at the closed clergy conference held at Garrison, New York, under the auspices of the Franciscan Friars of the Atonement, Graymoor.

Nihil Obstat: Edward A. Cerny, S.S., S.T.D.
Censor Librorum

Imprimatur: ✠ Lawrence J. Shehan, D.D.
Archbishop of Baltimore

October 26, 1962

The *Nihil Obstat* and *Imprimatur* are official declarations that a book or pamphlet is free of doctrinal or moral error. No implication is contained therein that those who have granted the *Nihil Obstat* and *Imprimatur* agree with the opinions expressed.

PRINTED IN THE UNITED STATES OF AMERICA BY
GRAYMOOR PRESS, PEEKSKILL, NEW YORK

Dedicated to

The Reverend Charles Boyer, S.J.

recipient of the 1961

Father Paul of Graymoor Award

"in recognition of

his distinguished contributions

in the field of Christian Unity"

Foreword

by Augustine Cardinal Bea

The great concern for Unity has made gigantic strides, especially among Catholics, from the moment the Vicar of Christ on earth himself announced a Council. Although the Council is not directly a Council of Unity, it must nevertheless with its very being constitute a kindly invitation to seek again that unity which Jesus so ardently implored. At this word of the Supreme Pontiff, the entire Christian world became alert to hear and to act for a more sincere and ardent quest for Unity. Indeed, we are not dealing with an objective whose complete realization is near, but even so, it is no less urgent to carry on the work with ardor and energy, inspired by the very Divine Heart of the Founder of the Church. The time is very propitious; the eyes of the world are turned upon the Christians; a great and unique occasion is offered them for displaying the unifying and pacifying force of Christianity, that is, of Christ, and of His Holy Spirit.

I congratulate all who collaborate in this conference, and any others who make known the importance and urgency of Unity work, and strive in every way to make all Catholics understand the great heart of the Vicar of Christ, John XXIII, gloriously reigning, a heart which is open to all those who bear the name of Christ on their brow, and which is so anxious to do all in its power that there be one Fold and one Shepherd, and that all be one as Jesus is with His Father.

This is my greeting and my wish. In this sense I shall gladly pray that your conference be a great success and add increment to Unity work in the United States. In the same spirit, on my part, I recommend to the prayers of all the work of the Secretariat for Unity that it may fulfill the great task entrusted to it by the Holy Father, and bring to the Council a useful contribution toward the great question of Christian Unity.

Augustine Cardinal Bea
Via Aurelia, 527, Rome
April 25, 1961

Contents

Catholic Ecumenism

by Msgr. J. G. M. Willebrands

The announcement of the Ecumenical Council made by Pope John XXIII on the memorable day of January 25, 1959 aroused a great new movement within the Catholic Church, took the whole of Christendom by surprise, and created new expectations for the future.

In his first announcement the Pope explicitly mentioned our separated brethren and expressed his hope that the Council should be an invitation to all who earnestly desire that unity for which Christ prayed so ardently from his Father. At first this fact even raised the question of whether the Pope had used the word *ecumenical* in the sense now given to it outside the Catholic Church. Especially in the non-Catholic world, the announcement was related to those desires and efforts for unity which have sprung from so many Christian communities, and which have led to the foundation of the World Council of Churches.

It is not surprising that non-Catholic Christians understood the words of the Holy Father in different ways, since the word *ecumenical* is used by them generally in a context and with a meaning which is determined by the ecclesiological concept proper to the different communities and churches that are affiliated to the World Council of Churches. The World Council in itself is not a Church or a super-Church (Dr. Visser 't Hooft has rejected this idea very clearly), but only a *council* or *fellowship* of churches. It respects the ecclesiology of all member churches, and wishes to serve the cause of unity without offending the stand of any member church. (Cf. the Toronto Declaration of the Central Committee of the World Council of Churches in 1950: it "does not prejudge the ecclesiological problem.") Nevertheless, I think it is not quite accurate to say that the World Council of Churches is ecclesiologically neutral. Without any doubt the World Council of Churches is not indifferent whether the cause of unity of all Christians, and in the first place of their own members, progresses or not; and it has developed definite ideas on the means and the methods by which it promotes the work of unity.

It is the particular task of the Faith and Order Commission to present the importance of visible Christian unity as the decisive ecumenical concern in all the activities of the World Council of Churches, and to clarify theologically what revelation contains on the real and concrete form of unity which the Lord willed for his Church. At a meeting of the Faith and Order Commission at St. Andrews, Scotland, and at the following session of the Central Committee of the World Council of Churches, this work of Faith and Order came clearly to the fore. Professor d'Espine summarized the results of the theological reflection of the last years of the Faith and Order Commission.

Moreover, the World Council of Churches is convinced that all practical activities—for instance, aid to people undergoing rapid social change, aid to refugees, relief for famines and epidemics—can be done in common by all Christians for the benefit of all men as a witness of Christian charity. In this field of applied Christian ethics, Christians can make it clear to the world how far they are already united. With the grace of God, this common witness may help them to come to a better understanding of each other, and to grow in unity. Dr. Visser 't Hooft expressed himself at the Central Committee meeting in Nyberg Strand in this way: "the whole life of the Churches is subjected to the creative activity of the Spirit." Nobody knows whither this Creating Spirit will lead them. The members of the World Council of Churches generally accept the necessity of arriving at a visible unity, but some of them conceive this unity as a federative unity in which differences of faith, worship, and church government remain, whereas others conceive the visibility as not being given by the Lord, especially as regards its structural or hierarchical elements.

Since none of the constituent churches are ecclesiologically neutral, the Council as a whole cannot be ecclesiologically neutral, even though it has no ecclesiology of its own. Its whole work is directed towards a future unity which it does not yet perceive, but in which it believes. In this belief it listens for the motions of the Holy Spirit and tries to find its way towards unity.

The expectation of many non-Catholics after the announcement of the Holy Father was that the Catholic Church would join them in their search for this unity. Not only non-Catholics, but also some Catholics at first explained the words of the Holy Father in an analogous way. They may have been led to this because of the high estimation which the Church (in the Instruction of the Holy Office, *Ecclesia Catholica* 20 Dec. 1949) expressed for the ecumenical movement of the separated brethren in the well known words: "The present time has witnessed in different parts of the world a growing desire amongst many people outside the Church for the reunion of all who believe in Christ the Lord. This may be attributed, under the inspiration of the Holy Ghost, to external factors and the changing attitude of men's minds, but above all to the united prayers of the faithful." And further, "they will forfeit none of the good that the grace of God has hitherto wrought in their souls." But it is one thing to appreciate the spiritual good found as a good of the Holy Ghost outside full visible communion with the Church, and quite another to use the word *ecumenical* in a sense which is not defined by Catholic ecclesiology, especially in a classical context, as is the term "Ecumenical Council."

What is the meaning of *ecumenical* and *oikoumene*? This poses the question not only of the meaning of a word, but of the whole position which we adopt as Catholics regarding the ecumenical movement; or perhaps it is a question of the clarification of the proper task and contribution of Catholics to the totality of the ecumenical movement. In all Christian communities, the meaning of the word *ecumenical* is determined by its own ecclesiology; so is it also for us.

The word *oikoumene* means literally the *whole inhabited world.* We can think of the political world, for instance the empire of Cyrus, or of Alexander the Great, or of the Emperor Augustus (cf Luke 2:1 where the census of the *oikoumene* decreed by the Emperor Augustus is mentioned). Or we can consider the world inhabited by man taken in its totality (the cosmos); in the Bible, the world is mostly used according to this second meaning. *Oikoumene* in the Bible is the inhabited world over which God has dominion because it belongs to him (Ps. 24:1), and which he will judge with justice when the anointed of Jehovah shall reign from sea to sea, from the Euphrates to the confines of the *oikoumene* (Ps. 72:8). According to Genesis 2:15, man is created to inhabit the whole world in acknowledgement of God's dominion. If man accomplishes this task according to the will of God, then God would reign over the world in and through man, and thus the world would proclaim the glory of God. This would result in peace on earth, the peace of Paradise. On the contrary, if the inhabitation and the cultivation of the world by man diverged from the will and the wisdom of God, then chaos would enter into the world and disturb the original goodness of both man and world. Man and world are comrades, bound together in a common destiny, whether felicitous or disastrous.

It was the original intention of the Creator to form an *oikoumene* that would be inhabited only by men of good will. From the beginning man and world have been placed in the way of that *oikoumene* which will find its achievement at the end of the world in a new heaven and a new earth where there will be no suffering and no death. In this growing *oikoumene*, sin and Satan gain power, but the Creator remains faithful to his eternal plan. He gathers out of sinful men a people which in the community of the Covenant will inhabit the world in justice and peace as a true servant of Jehovah. This people of God is the Church of Jehovah; it is open to the whole of humanity, and therefore is destined to be the Church of the *oikoumene*.

This Church was realized already in Our Lord Jesus Christ, who is therefore the peace of man and world. He is the Head of the new humanity, holding power over all that is in heaven, on the earth, and beneath the earth. His purpose is to collect, in the force of his spirit, his visible people around his visible representatives. His reign manifests itself in them, and in them a beginning of his peace is given to the world. The whole world is called to participation in this peace, which is of its nature cosmic.

Sinful division penetrated within this inhabited world. Thus originated the struggle about the nature of *ecumenicity,* since phenomenologically the situation of the Church in relation to the whole of mankind does not accord with her theological prerogative. From this discrepancy issues the ecumenical problem, and the ecumenical movement; and in this problem the whole inhabited world is involved.

On the non-Catholic side (with the exception of the Orthodox) one finds a conviction that the ecumenical Church lost her visible unity and must find it again. In this special context, the word *ecumenical* indicates the attitude of Christians who are divided and are in search of the restoration of this visible unity, whose future form cannot be foreseen.

In the Catholic world one finds the certitude that the one ecumenical Church, a gift of the Lord, is always present, although men in their limitations, often in their sinful narrowness, have in some measure obscured its ecumenical nature. This gift of the Lord exists in the fulness of grace and truth which was given at Pentecost to the visible community gathered around the Apostles. This gift cannot be lost to the Church but it might be in some way wanting in its human components. The essence of the Church consists precisely in the everlasting presence of this gift. The Church is the New Testament People of God which is allowed to participate in the fulness of grace and truth of the Lord present within it. Since this fulness is destined to all men, on the one hand, the Church is the *oikoumene,* possessing the spirit of truth; on the other hand, as the *oikoumene,* she is always in the state of becoming, in the sense that she is always introducing the whole world into the Kingdom of God.

The foundation of the Church as the *oikoumene* is her possession of Christ's fulness. She is the pleroma of Christ. It may also be said that the foundation of the Church as the *oikoumene* is her catholicity. The predicate *Catholic* is not Scriptural. We know it from the Apostles' Creed, and from the early Fathers. It belongs to the heritage of tradition. *Catholic* means the wholeness, the fulness, the unity in diversity, in which every part receives its meaning and reason for existence not from itself but from the whole—in such a way that it develops its own perfection within the context of the whole. This catholicity has been given to the Church in opposition to heresy (according to Clement of Alexandria). As a unity in a diversity, or in a plurality, she is the opposite of a monolith. She is world-embracing, or ecumenical. The Church is catholic because she contains the principle which is the perfection of every creature, the Alpha and the Omega, Jesus Christ who was sent by the Father (Col. 1:19,20).

The fulness of love comprises all God's divine attributes, including his power by which he perfects the world of Jew and Gentile. This fulness dwells everlastingly in Christ. The mystery of salvation, which St. Paul heralds, is the fact that in Christ the fulness of God dwells corporeally: corporeally because it dwells in him as the Head of the Body, and because we in communion with him share in that fulness (Col. 2: 9,10). In him all that is on earth and in heaven is reconciled and brought into unity. The Church, which is the Body of Christ, receives incessantly from him the fulness that he receives from the Father. This fulness reveals itself in her concrete form in all her parts. Just as a body has an organic structure, so has the Church's structure its hierarchically ordered parts. But everything finds its consistency in Christ (Eph. 4).

1. This hierarchical structure is the first way in which unity manifests itself in diversity. The Church manifests the fulness of the Lord in all her members. She is a priestly and royal people. She possesses the hierarchical order of a royal priesthood (I Cor. 12:28). This structure belongs to the wholeness and to the fulness which the Church received from her Lord. Ever since Pentecost, the Holy Spirit and the apostolic ministry have worked together to manifest the fulness of Christ by preaching and sanctifying. Not only did the apostles themselves act by virtue of the Holy Spirit, but the priests appointed by them were appointed by the Holy Spirit as guardians to govern the Church of God. The *Didache* asks that such bishops

and deacons be chosen who are worthy of the Lord, "for they fulfill among you the ministry of prophets and teachers" (Did. 15:1).

In Holy Scripture and in the early Fathers, it is clear that a community of the Lord is a visible community, which possesses a hierarchical structure. The submission of the members of the Church to her ministry is the proper means of their submission to the Head, Jesus Christ, and through him to the Father. In this hierarchical structure the diversity in unity of all is manifested. This idea we find particularly in the Epistles of St. Ignatius.

2. A second way in which the catholicity of the Church becomes manifest as the wholeness, or *pleroma,* is in its fulfillment of the Old Testament. The Church is the New Israel, who sings the songs of the kings and prophets; she sings them in a new way because their meaning has been revealed and fulfilled in Christ. The fathers of Israel drank from the spiritual rock that came after them and this Rock was Christ (I Cor. 10:4). They lived in the expectation of his coming. The Church is the fulfillment of their expectation because he was given to her as her Head. He is her fulness, she is his Body, full of him who fulfills all in all (Eph. 1:2-3).

3. In a third way the catholicity of the Church is seen under the aspect of the extension of the Church over the whole earth. As Cyril of Jerusalem writes: "We call the Church Catholic because she extends over the wide earth from end to end; because she teaches entirely and without error all the truths of salvation which men must know on visible and invisible things, on the things of heaven and earth; because she submits every generation to true worship, governors and governed, learned and unlearned; because she heals all sins, the sins of the body, and the sins of the spirit; and she possesses all kinds of virtue in work and in word, and in all spiritual gifts" (Catechesis 28-29).

The Church has the power to receive all men and all human values. She perfects the meaning of human existence and so she perfects the meaning of history through a recapitulation in Christ. This gathering together of all things in Christ does not signify totalitarianism. The Church respects and maintains the integrity of all that is proper to human values and legitimate human institutions. History, culture, juridical principles and science should not be curbed nor infringed upon, and the historical riches of our race should not be violated when they are received into the unity of Christ's Mystical Body. The miracle of tongues at the first Pentecost reveals her catholicity. "On that day was achieved in one what was announced to all. Already the whole Body of Christ speaks the languages of all, and it will speak the languages not yet spoken, for the Church will grow until it embraces all languages" (St. Augustine, *Ennarrationes in Psalmes,* 147:9).

In this description we see that the catholicity of the Church is a dynamic quality. Is this dynamism limited by the fact that the Church extends across all time, and over all nations? May we not say that she experiences also an *interior* growth by becoming more conscious of a certain fulness given her as she actualizes and lives in her history the mystery of salvation? Since she baptizes the men of all ages, she experiences within herself the development of problems, and the changes and transformations of human society. Nevertheless, the very reason of the Church's interior growth can never be an immanent human reason, whether psychological or social; the interior growth develops under the guidance of the Holy Spirit. We can summarize the Acts of the Apostles in this one text—"Now the Church had peace throughout all Judea and Galilee, and Samaria, and was edified, walking in the fear of the Lord, and was filled with the consolation of the Holy Ghost" (Acts 9:31).

In all the transformations in which the City of God struggles with the world, between the Ascension of the Lord and his Second Coming, the Spirit "will convince the world of sin, and justice and of judgment" (Jo. 16:8), and he will bring her to the fulness of truth (16:13). When Peter received the heathen into the Church it meant not only an extension of the number, and a new spreading over the earth. Indeed, a new awareness of Catholicity broke in upon the Church, a new dimension was opened to her, and a new insight was given into the Glad Tidings that Jesus Christ is the Lord of all.

The great process in which the Church undergoes development from the Alpha to the Omega, from the fulness in her initial state to the fulness of her completion at the end of time, is not the mere development of an abstract idea merely becoming more conscious of herself. The growth unto the measure of the age of the fulness of Christ (Eph. 4:13) is a development realized in a concrete historical situation. The Church is placed in the dynamism and development of history. Since a divine principle is present and at work within her, she never becomes historical in the sense that she could collapse in history as earthly things are born and die. She was not born from history and never will perish in history. She was prepared in history by the mission of the prophets, and she was realized in history by the mission of the Son of God. Although she remains and develops herself in history, in her is present a divine element which transcends history. Her nature and her development never can be measured with the earthly measure of progress and decline. In her history she knows periods of flourishing prosperity, and of diminished luster, but her development prescinds from all real historical facts because it is eschatological. She is the Kingdom of God in the period between the Alpha and the Omega. She possesses not only the prophecies which shall be made void, the tongues which shall cease, and knowledge which shall be destroyed, but she also possesses charity which will never fall away. At every moment of her existence she realizes in her concrete form the presence of the word of God in this world—veiled, but imperishable. The Church of future glory and the Church in her present state are one. Therefore, her development is eschatological.

Catholic ecumenism finds its origin and starting point in its divinely bestowed fulness, unity, and catholicity. In the present world situation, the Church is brought face to face with the tremendous problem of a divided Christendom. It is a problem which refers immediately to the Church's catholicity. In the last century there was a vast development of missionary activity. It doubtless enhanced the Church's catholicity with new splendor, but it was manifested principally by way of numerical increase, and wider geographical expansion. Interior enrichment and renewed consciousness of her own fulness was favored to a lesser degree by this admission of new peoples into the unity of her flock. These benefits are the expectation of the future. The newly created indigenous hierarchies prepare the ground for local Churches, and these will, with the passage of time, develop their particular character and splendor, and thus contribute to the glory of the whole.

The living encounter of Catholics with their separated brethren, which is a characteristic of our own generation, brings with it a new reflection upon the fulness of the mystery of salvation. May we not well suppose that the ecumenical movement in which the many Christians of different denominations work together for the cause of Christian unity has been a movement inspired by God? May not the Spirit of the Lord be drawing them together in this common effort for the purpose of reminding them of the true fulness and catholicity of the Church? The Instruction of the Holy Office allows us to discern in these developments the assistance of the Holy Ghost. But the Holy Ghost is ever at work for the benefit of Christ's Mystical Body, the Church.

Therefore we ask ourselves whether it could not be that while the movement of our separated brethren grows and advances, the Holy Ghost is simultaneously stimulating and inspiring the Church to a fuller manifestation, a greater development and consciousness of her own catholicity.

The succession of historical events which led to the separation of the Eastern Churches from the Church of Rome, and to the break-away of large Christian communities in the West, did not and could not affect the essential unity and catholicity of the Church. In fact, these separations, nevertheless, veiled its fuller manifestation and influenced its development. These great separations doubtless have occasioned a new reflection on our own faith and worship, but at the Council of Trent and during the Counter-Reformation period the Church was so much concerned with defining and preaching the true and safe doctrine to those who remained faithful to the Church that contact with the separated brethren was soon lost.

It is a new and renewing event that in our time the dialogue, the encounter with separated Christians, became a fact. In this dialogue we learn how to present the Church to the separated brethren as the *signum levatum in nationibus*. By this dialogue we learn his Christian questions, protests and concerns. For the first time since the separation of the sixteenth century we have a direct experience and knowledge of the theology and spirituality of our separated brethren.

Already the experience from direct encounter and dialogue has shown how our past knowledge of the separated brethren has been in so many ways faulty, even false. It seems to be against Christian charity not even to know one another, and how are we able to answer an authentic problem if we do not even know what the problem is.

The answer we must give is not simply to a theological or theoretical question, but to a question that rises out of the concrete religious situation of the Christian communities. Thus, in the direct encounter with our separated brethren we study not only their theological positions, but we learn to see and to appreciate the concrete expressions of their spiritual lives, their forms of prayer, their pastoral methods, and the actual functioning of their communities. As the Church herself finds the answers to the problems of modern life only by a direct contact with that life, so the problem of Christian unity can be solved only after a long, direct and concrete experience and awareness of the tragic situation before us—divided Christians and divided Christian communities.

Thus the separation of Christians can be an occasion for a new reflection on the way the Church can acquire a new self-consciousness and expression of her internal being. She will thus appear more clearly as the *Oikoumene* for all, in which the separated brethren can more easily see their true home.

On several occasions, Pope John XXIII spoke in this way of the importance of the Second Vatican Council for the promotion of Christian unity. For example, in his address to the Presidents of Italian Catholic Action, His Holiness stressed the necessity of internal renewal in the Church, and added: "then having accomplished this heavy task, having eliminated what, on the part of man, could prove an obstacle to speedy progress, we will present the Church in all its splendor and will say to our separated brethren, Orthodox, Protestant, etc.: 'See, brothers, here is the Church of Christ. We have striven to remain faithful to her.' "

More concretely the biblical and liturgical movement, already stirring within the Catholic Church, along with deepening developments in ecclesiology, will prove to be the best starting points of a renewal in the life of the Church to meet the needs of the separated brethren. These three movements were all authoritatively encouraged when Pope Pius XII sealed them in the form of three encyclicals, *Divino afflante spiritu* for the biblical movement, *Mediator Dei* for the liturgical renewals; and *Mystici Corporis* for ecclesiological studies. We all hope that the Second Vatican Council will give further impetus to these movements by issuing clear and up-to-date directives for the whole Church on how to present herself to the whole world, and especially in the encounter with separated Christians.

The proper object of Catholic ecumenism is always to grow in Catholicity and unity, in service to the separated brethren by the very encounter and dialogue itself. Although the separation of Christians must be an occasion for new reflection and renewing efforts in the Church, this fact of facing a divided Christianity is not the ultimate reason for it.

The deepest reason is to be found in the command to manifest in our Christian lives the glory of the Lord. By the sanctification of our life, we give witness to the world of the work of the redemption of Christ. And we have to fulfill this command, independently of whether there is a separation of Christians or not. We never can forget that with the imperishable gift of fullness there remains at the same time the obligation to actualize this gift at every moment of history and in a form adapted to the needs of our time.

The Catholic ecumenical movement then, is primarily internal to the Church. It is an internal development, played in a dialogue with the world which is separated from and outside of the Church. This internal movement is a *metanoia*, the conversion not of others but of ourselves. It concerns the readjustment of all that has gone awry in our own Christian thinking, speaking and living. It has to do with the unveiling of what has been obscured, by our own sins, in the course of time.

We hope it is clear from all this that there can be no opposition between ecumenical work and what is called conversion work, that is, the entrance of individuals into the Church. We acknowledge fully the vocation by which the Spirit calls an individual to the Church. The ecumenical movement can give guidance and instruction, if such a vocation becomes clear, and especially if this individual comes from another Christian community.

The ecumenical movement serves the Church by providing the convert not only with the best doctrinal explanation but also with that richness of spirituality as it is incorporated in the Church. In other words, to find himself at home, to find his own place in the House of the Father.

I would like to suggest areas which need a re-evaluation and renewed consciousness by giving fuller expression to:

1. The episcopacy in its relation to the papacy, in the structure of the Church.

2. The universal priesthood of the faithful, and consequently, the importance of personal conviction of faith, with its apostolic orientation—not only an intellectual understanding of the faith, but a personal conviction that gives witness to it.

3. The Church as the New Israel, the continuation, and perfect fulfillment of the Old Covenant.

4. The Kingdom of Christ over men and over the whole cosmos, and Christian hope as embracing the expectation of the Second Coming.

5. The Word of God in the Church: the Word of God not only as the foundation of divine truth, but as the Word of God by which he reveals and gives himself to us as the nourishing Bread of life. In this way we receive the Word of God in the Liturgy, especially the Eucharist. By this Word of God preaching should be inspired more than generally is the case.

6. The fostering of the reading of the Bible as the source of personal spiritual life.

7. The role of Church hymns, with hymns in the vernacular, as we find cultivated in other Christian communities. It is

a pity that our most beautiful hymns are all in Latin (*Adoro te, Veni Sancte Spiritus*), and that we have not a development of our hymns in the vernacular as do other Christian communities (Bach, Wesley, etc.).

8. A liturgical formation by which the active participation of the faithful, already inculcated by the words and spirit of Pius X, will become more factual.

9. A collaboration with our separated brethren in relief work and in reforming profane institutions in a Christian spirit. In this collaboration it is possible to give to the materialistic world, in a certain limited but real way, a common Christian witness, in which it will be manifest that a certain measure of common bonds always exists among Christians.

The Bible and Reunion

by Walter M. Abbott, S.J.

For many years, Catholic and Protestant biblical scholars have given the divided Christian world a good example of practical co-operation. The impression has sometimes been given that this co-operation dates back only to 1943, when Pope Pius XII brought out his great encyclical on biblical studies, *Divino afflante spiritu.*[1] In that letter the Pontiff urged Catholic scholars to "neglect none of those discoveries, whether in the domain of archaeology or in ancient history or literature, which serve to make better known the mentality of the ancient writers as well as their manner and art of reasoning, narrating and writing."[2] It is true that this was official approbation of an open approach to work done mainly by non-Catholics, but, as the Pope knew, Catholic scholars had already a tradition of gathering truth and light wherever it might be found.

The tradition of using secular knowledge in the defense of religious truth goes back as far as the time of the Fathers of the Church. St. Augustine called it "taking spoils of the Egyptians."

The thrust of nineteenth century Rationalism put the scholars of the Church on the defensive, but not long after this period Catholic scholars were quarrying again in the archaeological reports, lexicons and critical works of Protestant scholars.

---

[1]The encyclical, dated September 30, 1943, was published in *Acta Apostolicae Sedis,* vol. XXXV (October 20, 1943), pp. 297-325. For an English translation, see *The Catholic Mind,* vol. XLII (May, 1944), pp. 257-283.

[2]*Ibid.*: *AAS,* p. 317; *Catholic Mind,* p. 176.

Even before Pius XII's encyclical appeared in 1943, no serious Old Testament scholar would write about the Psalms without consulting the important work of the Lutherans, Hermann Gunkel and S. Mowinckel.[3] No New Testament scholar would attempt to discuss the language of the Gospels and Epistles without consulting the dictionary begun by the Protestant G. Kittel.[4]

Since World War II, newspaper and magazine articles have been informing the public in general about the constantly increasing co-operation between biblical scholars of the different churches. The scholars themselves had long known how much in agreement they were on the objective facts of archaeology. They knew that they had to use the same lexicons for the ancient languages and that they had to agree on the evidence of their eyes when they scanned the lines of ancient manuscripts. The work that has been done on the Qumran Scrolls, or "Dead Sea Scrolls," has dramatically illustrated the objective and scientific approach prevalent among biblical scholars of different faiths.

Catholic and non-Catholic scholars worked as a team under the direction of the Dominican scholar Roland de Vaux, piecing together and translating fragments of more than 500 manuscripts from the newly-discovered libraries of the ancient Essene settlement near the Dead Sea. The team included an agnostic scholar, John M. Allegro; a priest from the Archdiocese of Bordeaux, M. l'abbé Maurice Baillet; another Dominican priest, Pierre Benoit; Frank M. Cross, Jr., Presbyterian minister and professor at Harvard University; a minister of the Evangelical Church, Göttingen, Dr. Claus-Hunno Hunzinger; a refugee priest from the Archdiocese of Warsaw, Jozef T. Milik; Msgr. Patrick W. Skehan, from the Catholic University of America; a priest from the Archdiocese of Paris, M. l'abbé Jean Starcky; a

---

[3]An excellent essay by A.R. Johnson, "The Psalms," in *The Old Testament and Modern Study: A Generation of Discovery and Research,* edited by H.H. Rowley (Oxford University Press, 2nd impression, 1952), pp. 162-209, outlines the importance of the work done by Gunkel and others.

[4]G. Kittel (ed.), *Theologisches Wörterbuch zum Neuen Testament* (Stuttgart: W. Kohlhammer, 1933–).

Protestant scholar from Jesus College, Oxford University, John Strugnell. To this group were temporarily attached Rev. Raymond E. Brown, S.S., from St. Mary's Seminary in Baltimore; William Oxtoby, a Protestant scholar from Princeton University; and Rev. Joseph A. Fitzmyer, S.J., from Woodstock College in Maryland. This was practical co-operation on a large scale at the highest level of scholarship.

Besides agreeing on what the texts of the scrolls say, these scholars have been able to furnish material that pretty nearly settles some old disputes. Until the study of the scrolls, some commentators on the Bible held that St. John's Gospel was written against the theological background of pagan Greek culture rather than that of Palestine and Jewish culture. Now it is clearly seen that concepts found in St. John's Gospel—for example the theological symbolism of light and darkness—were to be found in theological writings composed in Palestine during the time of Christ.

A number of Catholic biblical scholars are engaged in communicating the best of modern biblical research, like this work on the Dead Sea scrolls, to priests at symposiums or summer institutes in order that busy pastors of souls may keep up, to some extent, with developments in biblical scholarship. The fruits of modern research are being communicated to the students in seminaries and colleges throughout the country. There is now more and more widespread knowledge about the literary forms of Genesis, the conventions or ways of expression that must be discerned in the Psalms in order to appreciate their full importance, and the proper approach to the Gospels. Protestant ministers gather at several places for symposiums and institutes like those of the Catholic priests. Much of the teaching in Protestant schools and colleges shows the same results of modern literary, historical and archaeological work on the Bible.

Agreement on objective literary and historical facts about the Bible has mounted up so considerably that a number of observers are encouraged to feel that in biblical studies we may have the most promising groundwork for movements toward union or reunion in the Christian world. Cardinals and bishops of the Catholic Church have made statements along these lines on a number of occasions.[5] Protestant prelates and ministers have often spoken in the same vein. All of these churchmen know that it is difficult to overcome a polemical tradition that is more than four hundred years old. But they have been encouraged by the fact that clergymen and scholarly laymen of the various churches actually seem to be doing it by working together in societies of Old Testament and New Testament studies. In Europe, Catholic bishops and Protestant prelates have been hosts to these meetings for some years now. In recent years, we have seen this development in the United States, too. The conferences at Wayne State University in Detroit, for example, have had as co-chairmen a bishop of the Protestant Episcopal Church, a Catholic monsignor and a Jewish rabbi. It is felt more and more that, under the guidance of the Holy Spirit, this kind of co-operation could be ideal ground on which to build a road to unity.

Catholic and Protestant Biblical scholars are writing for one another's learned journals. One Catholic scholar, writing in the nondenominational *Journal of Biblical Literature*,[6] has stated that "unanimity in textual criticism, in historical investigation, in exegesis, and even in a theological synthesis of the Bible is theoretically independent of confessional differences." The author seemed to think that if Catholic scholars continue in the path in which they have set out "there must be the happy result of a wider and more friendly communication in scholarship." This, he added, would not be a step toward ecumenical union, but it would be a welcome step toward better human relations, and this should have a salutary effect on "our heterogeneous society."

There is certainly a scholarly, irenic tone at meetings of the interdenominational Society of Biblical Literature and Exegesis. At the 1959 national meeting, a Jewish scholar, Dr. Robert Gordis, read a paper in which he criticized certain elements in a theory about the language of the Book of Koheleth (Ecclesiastes) advanced in an article by a Catholic priest, M.J. Dahood,

---

[5]Cf. Walter M. Abbott, S.J., *The Bible . . . Road to Unity* (New York: America Press, 1961), p. 1 ff.

[6]John L. McKenzie, S.J., "Problems of Hermeneutics in Roman Catholic Exegesis," *JBL*, vol. LXXVII, Part III (September, 1958), pp. 197-204.

S.J. A Methodist layman, Dr. William F. Albright, calmly and objectively argued against Dr. Gordis' points in the discussion which followed. A Baptist professor of Scripture sitting next to me remarked: "We're all just scholars here at a meeting like this, Father." Catholic priests and Protestant ministers have shared official positions in the regional organizations of the Society. Protestant biblical scholars, e.g., Dr. Albright and Prof. Oscar Cullmann, have been invited to lecture at Catholic seminaries, and Catholic biblical scholars have been guest lecturers at Protestant institutions. Scholars of different churches applauded the appointment of R.A.F. MacKenzie, S.J., to lecture at the University of Minnesota in 1960. Similar acclaim greeted the appointment of David Stanley, S.J., to a three-year professorship at the University of Iowa. Every other year, Catholic, Protestant and Jewish biblical scholars meet in a biblical history symposium at Loyola University in Chicago. The spectacle of such joint efforts to achieve a meeting of minds is proof that friendly exchange and understanding are really developing in our pluralistic society.

Dr. Albright has been one of the main reasons for the increasing agreement among biblical scholars in this country. He is a leading expert in Semitic studies. For more than forty years, his approach as a teacher and scholar has been primarily literary and historical, and he has on a number of occasions expressed the view that "there can be nothing but unanimity of opinion in biblical matters whenever it is a question of scientific methods and historical criticism."[7] So esteemed and trusted is he by authorities of the various churches that many of the future professors of Sacred Scripture were sent to do part of their studies under his direction at Johns Hopkins University.

Co-operation of Catholic and Protestant biblical scholars, especially in the discernment of literary forms in books of the Bible, has resulted in some definite conclusions and a number of interesting theories. It used to be that this kind

(April, 1959), pp. 198-199.

[7]See, for example, the account of Dr. Albright's lectures at the Paulist Center in Boston, Mass., in *The Catholic Biblical Quarterly,* vol. XXI

of work was carried on in the professional journals and then filtered out through the seminary professors to the students. Now, however, when some interesting theory is proposed in a learned article, there is often a report in the newspapers the very next day. The speed and the scope of modern communications complicate, and to some extent sabotage, scholarly processes. The newspapers drop into parishes everywhere a number of ideas for which pastors and people are not prepared. A scholar may have compared biblical passages with other contemporary pieces of writing and suggested that a certain Semitic way of speaking has been used, with the result that perhaps the passages are metaphorical and symbolic rather than factual narrative. When they read about it in their papers, the people and some of their pastors are disturbed; they wonder if there has been tampering with the Sacred Scriptures.

An important article in *Theological Studies*[8] presents a study of the Parable of the Sower and its explanation in order to show what careful linguistic and historical research can reveal in the biblical books. It shows how well-founded that research is. It shows also the kind of thing which permits scholars like Dr. Albright to observe that in literary and historical studies of the Bible there must be agreement.

Francis J. McCool, S.J., professor at the Pontifical Biblical Institute in Rome, entitled his article "The Preacher and the Historical Witness of the Gospels," because he wished to help priests who are some years away from their seminary courses to catch up on more recent developments in the field of scriptural studies and the understanding of the Bible. Many a parishioner these days wants to know more, too, because articles and stories have appeared in mass media indicating that the Bible must be read "in a new way" and that the Gospels are not so easily understood as one might think.

Fr. McCool writes that the Greek vocabulary of the Parable of the Sower points unmistakably to a Semitic background; all indications, in fact, point to an Aramaic original. From the style

[8]Francis J. McCool, S.J., "The Preacher and the Historical Witness of the Gospels," *TS*, vol. 21 (December, 1960), pp. 517-543.

and context, biblical historians can date the parable to some time near the close of Jesus' ministry in Galilee.

The explanation of the parable (Mark 4:13-21), however, uses words and expressions which are not to be found in Gospel texts that are clearly the actual words of Jesus. The language is like what we find in the New Testament Epistles; in other words, it is like the language of the early Church. Unlike the parable itself, the explanatory passage contains no Semitisms and does not hint that it is "translation Greek" from an Aramaic original.

Also, the explanation of the parable is clumsy compared to the parable itself. The classes of listeners are likened to the seeds that fall on the various parts of the field—"And those likewise who are sown on the rocky ground are they who . . ." —whereas what clearly is meant is that they are like the different kinds of soil in which the seed is placed. Finally, the simple parable is made out to be an allegory, i.e., all the details, cryptically expressed in metaphorical language, are interpreted one by one.

Biblical scholars commonly hold today that the explanation of the parable in verses 13-20 is a piece of catechetical teaching from the first decades of the Church. Their reasons are not of the "would have" or "must have" variety that are sometimes advanced to support mere theory. In this case they are dealing with philological facts. One conclusion that intelligent readers of Fr. McCool's article will immediately reach is that those who know the biblical languages are in a much better position to talk about the meaning of biblical texts than those who use only translations.

To read the Gospels as if they were merely straightforward history as we know it today is, in fact, to treat the sacred books the way nineteenth century German historians (von Ranke, Mommsen, Meyer) treated official records of European history—as "pure" historical sources, i.e., precise, detailed and objective. Fr. McCool recounts how that German influence led to the search for the "Jesus of history" and to the view that the Gospels are "contaminated" by theological interpretations.

Gradually, however, it has become clear that some parts of the Gospels were written later than others, and that there are various forms of literary approach in the Sacred Books. Fr. McCool writes:

> Since none of these forms intend to express the event or saying to which they bear witness in strictly historical statement, as that phrase is understood today, the historian must determine the precise intention implicit in the original form and that revealed by the particular use which the Evangelist has made of it. This done, he must decide the extent to which these two distinct intentions have influenced the statement in his text, and in the light of these considerations judge exactly what can be deduced from it concerning the event or saying in the life of our Lord which is being reported. This is a delicate business, which can be safely accomplished only by a formed historian who has been trained in the evaluation of ancient texts generally and of the Gospel texts in particular.[9]

What this means in practice becomes immediately evident if one looks at the Rev. Gerard S. Sloyan's commentary on Mark's chapter 4: "...Jesus has left the way open for allegory. What the inspired teacher Mark does with it is surely in his spirit, if not nearly as clever as the first telling by the Master."[10]

Why did the early Church so restate Jesus' Parable of the Sower that his word (the Christian revelation) replaced the kingdom of God as the center of interest? The answer is that the sacred writer was not envisaging in the explanatory passage the Jewish audience to which Jesus first addressed the parable with its germinal form of his teaching about the kingdom. Mark stresses, rather, the difficulties experienced by his contemporaries in putting into practice what the Christian revelation demanded of them.

The transposition does not falsify the original meaning of the parable. There is a shift in stress because of the change of audience, but both parable and interpretation implicitly call for a change in the hearers' attitude toward Jesus or his word. As Fr. McCool points out, the modern historian does not find

---

[9]*Ibid.*, pp. 529-530.

[10]*New Testament Reading Guide*: *The Gospel of St. Mark*. Introduction and commentary by Gerard S. Sloyan (Collegeville, Minn.: The Liturgical Press, 1960), p. 39.

anything in this procedure which he would term "unhistorical," because he is prepared to "allow the Evangelists within limits to establish their own norms for historical writing, instead of imposing on them those of his own time and place."[11]

The objective literary and historical approach that we have seen in Fr. McCool's article is the kind of thing that has brought Catholic and non-Catholic biblical scholars closer and closer in agreement. The quest on both sides is the same: to discern the meaning that the biblical authors originally intended to convey. It is the message which God inspired in the prophets, in Paul, in the apostolic preaching that reputable scholars of all faiths desire to unfold to the people with utmost accuracy. They carry on their work for the people of God knowing, as Pope Pius XII put it, that it is perfectly proper to hope they can contribute something toward the deeper and more accurate information on some matters than commentators of old had.[12] They carry on their work in a spirit described by Pope John XXIII, who told biblical scholars at the Golden Jubilee of the Pontifical Biblical Institute in Rome that they must discover and make known to all the truths that are contained in the Bible.[13]

Discovery, or rediscovery, of biblical truths sometimes involves peeling off interpretations that seem to be traditional but are really the result of mistaken historical and literary approaches to the Bible. We have just seen that Catholic and Protestant scholars alike can prove that what seemed to be chronological passages of one day's events in the Gospels are rather literary compilations and combinations made, after the events described, by the first bishops of the Church under the inspiration of the Holy Spirit. It is becoming clearer and clearer, therefore, that the distinction between Scripture and the Church must be re-examined. Scholars who are faithful to the objective results of biblical study should come more and more to appreciate the essential interrelationship of Spirit, Church and Scrip-

---

[11]Francis J. McCool, S.J., *op. cit.*, p. 341.

[12]Pius XII, *op. cit.*, *AAS*, XXXV, p. 313; *Catholic Mind*, p. 272.

[13]John XXIII, *Allocutio die* 17 *Februarii mensis a.* 1960, *AAS*, vol. LII (March 29, 1960), pp. 152-158.

ture. This cannot fail to have considerable effect upon the ecumenical movement.

Deeper study of the apostolic preaching contained in the Bible and the authoritative use made in that preaching of the earlier revealed word of God often leads Protestants to look for the continuation of that preaching and authority promised by Christ. When they look about in the modern world and find what they seek in the Catholic Church, they embrace in the Church Christ still preaching and authoritatively interpreting the Sacred Scriptures. Along the way, whether they find this joyful outcome or not, they often make considerable advances in history, archaeology and linguistics. Catholic scholars have long been aware of these facts, but since Pope Pius XII directed, in 1943, that they take advantage of all such advances, they have more generously adopted the solid scientific work of their Protestant colleagues. As a result, Brendan McGrath, O.S.B., declared in his presidential address to the Catholic Biblical Association of America that progress in Catholic biblical scholarship was due "in no small measure" to the "altogether admirable willingness" of Catholic scholars to avail themselves of the "assured results" and "fruitful labors" of Protestant scholars.[14] There is surely a working out of divine providence in all of this. Protestants are encouraged by the open approach of Catholics, and Catholics are enriched by the objective contributions of Protestants.

As the Benedictine scholar pointed out in his address, there is no question for Catholic scholars of any compromise of defined Catholic faith. He put the case quite simply with these concluding lines:

> The goal is what it has always been for genuine Scripture studies, to come to know ever more perfectly and completely what the Word of God is saying to us. And if we can make any progress toward that goal with the assistance of a suggestion of Gregory of Nyssa or Theodore of Mopsuestia, of Maimonides or Luther, of Lagrange or Bultmann, or anyone else, so much

[14] Brendan McGrath, O.S.B., unpublished text, quoted in Walter M. Abbott, S.J., "The Bible Is a Bond," *America*, vol. 102 (October 24, 1959), p. 100.

the better, for it is truth that we are after and God is in no way limited with regard to the manner in which He condescends to make His truth known to us.[15]

The spectacle of such detached and objective pursuit of truth is bound to inspire imitation in other fields where Catholics and Protestants can profitably work together, for example, the whole field of biblical theology. In the spirit of the pontificate of Pope John XXIII, that is the way it ought to be.

It would help matters considerably if there were a translation of the Bible to which both Catholics and Protestants could refer in their discussions. When the proposal for a common translation in English was advanced in *America,*[16] the author had in mind the possibility of ending the different numberings of the Psalms, the different spellings of biblical names. Among the many practical advantages of the resulting harmony there would be, one could hope, considerable improvement in the psychological approach wherever Catholics and Protestants were working together, not only in biblical and theological studies but also in the wider ecumenical discussions. The proposal was intended to be of some help in healing the breach caused by the Reformation.

It was a new translation that the author of the article had in mind, not the adoption of any existing translation. Dom Bernard Orchard, O.S.B., and Dom Edmund Flood, O.S.B., were in favor of having the Catholic Church adopt the Revised Standard Version.[17] They felt that a Catholic edition of the RSV could be worked out since "the number of actual changes deemed necessary to make its text conform to Catholic theology and Scriptural usage would . . . seem, according to the investigations of a recent committee of Catholic scholars, to amount to less than a score." The author of the *America* article did not back this proposal. He discerned that many of the Catholic bishops and the Catholic people would feel there was too much

[15]*Ibid., loc. cit.*

[16]*Ibid.,* p. 102.

[17]Bernard Orchard, O.S.B., and Edmund Flood, O.S.B., "Sharing the Same Book," *Worship,* vol. XXXIII (August-September, 1959), pp. 530-536.

of an element of "surrender" in the idea of adopting or adapting an official Protestant version of the Bible. It seemed to him, also, that not many Protestants would welcome the idea of adopting or adapting an official Catholic translation. The only solution, he felt, would be to have a group of Catholic and non-Catholic scholars work out a new translation, which could then be approved by Catholic and non-Catholic ecclesiastical authorities. The new translation would not be the official book of one church as opposed to another; it would be, simply and objectively, *the* Bible.

F. F. Bruce, Rylands Professor of Biblical Criticism and Exegesis in the University of Manchester, England, discussed the proposal toward the end of a recently published book.[18] He began by observing that "any co-operation on an agreed translation might seem to be excluded by considerations of church politics." He found it "all the more interesting, then," that an article should be published in the American Roman Catholic journal *America* expressing the view that a common translation of the Bible "would be a great achievement in the history of Christianity." Professor Bruce thought that the author "may have been flying a kite in this article," but, he added, "it is significant that such a kite could be flown."

The idea of the "kite," it may now be told, was inspired by Robert A. Dyson, S.J., a professor of biblical exegesis for twenty years at the Pontifical Biblical Institute in Rome. For many years he had held that one of the most effective steps in the Christian unity movement in the English-speaking world would be the preparation of a unified Bible acceptable to both Protestants and Catholics. He firmly believed that modern scientific knowledge of ancient texts and languages had grown so greatly that a unified, scholarly, scientific presentation of the Word of God was entirely feasible. He used to say that there was not a single Protestant scholar who would not accept the idea of a unified Bible. He died, however, in 1959, without having written anything about the idea. It was partly in memory of him that the "kite" was sent aloft.

---

[18]F.F. Bruce, *The English Bible: A History of Translations* (New York: Oxford University Press, 1961), pp. 208-210.

The "kite" was also intended to stir the flight of a phoenix from the ashes in which it lay. As Father Dyson used to say, there are comparatively few irreconcilable differences in Protestant and Catholic interpretations of passages in the Bible, and these difficulties could be taken care of in footnotes accompanying the unified text. A group of British Catholic scholars actually secured permission from Bernard Cardinal Griffin, Archbishop of Westminster, to publish a commentary on the Bible that would present the Revised Standard Version as the text. Their plan called for revision of about twenty verses in that translation. The Cardinal died, however, before the project could be carried out.

It was this author's hope that a better bird could arise from the ashes. Father Dyson used to say: "If we are going to work for unity, one of the vital things is to have all Christian denominations using the same Bible." All would not use the Revised Standard Version, but perhaps all would use a new translation done by scholars of various faiths in the most objective manner possible and subsequently endorsed by church authorities.

The most promising hope for this purpose was, at one time, the New English Bible, sponsored jointly by the Oxford and Cambridge University Presses, with planning and direction furnished by representatives of practically all major Christian churches of the British Isles. If Catholic scholars had participated in the project, the translation of the New Testament which appeared in March, 1961, could have been the beginning of the common Bible that the English-speaking world needs.[19] Catholic scholars would, in fact, have been in the project were

[19]Thomas Corbishley, S.J., Superior of the Farm Street Church in London, England, wrote in the British Catholic weekly newspaper *The Universe* on March 17, 1961 (date of publication of the *NEB* New Testament): "Broadly speaking, it is safe to say that the new translation, based as it is on strict scholarship and not seeking to be 'the expression of any denominational or doctrinal leaning,' could at least serve as a basis for an agreed text." Some details of the translation, he added, would have to be modified to make it a Bible that Catholics could share in common with non-Catholics. Father Corbishley's proposal is very similar to proposals that have been made about the Revised Standard Version, and it will probably meet with the same psychological difficulties.

it not that the hierarchy had only a few years before adopted the version by Msgr. Ronald A. Knox as the official one for England and Wales. A good Catholic Bible had been provided for the Catholic people; the need of more than this was not then felt by the hierarchy.

In the meantime, however, Pope John XXIII has come upon the scene and kindled new interest in Christian unity. His new Secretariat for Promoting Christian Unity is directed, providentially, by one of the most respected biblical scholars of our times, Augustine Cardinal Bea. Bishops in France, Germany and the Netherlands have been impressed by the success of translations of the Bible made from the same critical editions of biblical manuscripts and accepted by both Catholics and non-Catholics.

The proposal that we seek a common English translation of Holy Scripture for all Christians was warmly received by Catholics and non-Catholics, churchmen and scholars, and it created widespread interest among the people. Robert M. Grant, president of the Society of Biblical Literature and Exegesis, expressed the feelings of many when he wrote that it would be "hard to overestimate" the importance of such an agreed version of the Bible as a "unifying force" among Christians. Nevertheless, there were some pockets of opposition in the English-speaking world.[20]

There were some who felt it would be better to wait until three current translation projects were completed—the Catholic Confraternity translation, the Protestant Oxford-Cambridge translation, and a translation of the Hebrew text by Jewish scholars. Some of those who had sponsored and directed the recently completed Revised Standard Version were understandably reluctant to turn their attention to another project. A few of the scholars engaged in the unfinished translation projects were uneasy about what they felt might be a threat to the success of their project. One or two voices were raised to suggest that a common English translation would "impoverish" or "water

[20]J. Coert Rylaarsdam joined Dr. Grant in signing the statement. See the fuller text quoted in Walter M. Abbott, S.J., "The Bible Is a Bond," *op. cit.*, p. 102.

down" the message of the Scriptures. A few scholars questioned whether a common translation could be made successfully. A few doubted that such a translation was desirable.

Amid the general desire and hope and the scattered doubts, this writer learned that Dr. Albright and David Noel Freedman had set out on their own to produce a new translation of the entire Bible with the help of a team of Protestant, Jewish and Catholic scholars.[21] They were not working under the auspices of any church or group of churches. Each scholar was to do an objective job with the book or books assigned to him. If the scholars engaged in the work were of the first rank and their translation turned out to be thoroughly accurate, might it not be possible to petition the various churches' approval upon completion of the work? Was it not legitimate to hope that this great work of combined Catholic, Protestant and Jewish scholarship could turn out to be the common Bible we needed for theological and ecumenical discussions?

As Dr. Albright and Dr. Freedman assembled their team, it became clear that they were gathering the cream of modern scholars.[22] The way they and their colleagues are going about

---

[21]Cf. Walter M. Abbott, S.J., "A Bible Reader for Public Schools," *America*, vol. 104 (October 22, 1960), p. 118; "A Common Bible Reader for Public Schools," *Religious Education*, vol. LVI (January-February, 1961), p. 23.

[22]The roster of scholars and their assignments is as follows:
W.F. Albright and D.N. Freedman (Book of Exodus); Bernhard Anderson (Minor Prophets I); John Bright (Book of Jeremiah); Raymond E. Brown, S.S. (Gospel of John and Epistles of John); Edward F. Campbell (Megillot Scrolls: Ruth, Esther, Song of Songs); Frank M. Cross and D.N. Freedman (Books of Samuel and Kings); Mitchell Dahood, S.J. (Psalms); W.D. Davies (Gospels of Mark and of Matthew); David Flusser (Epistle to the Hebrews); J.L. Ginsberg (Book of I Isaiah); Moshe Greenberg (Book of Ezekiel); Walter Harrelson (Minor Prophets II); Louis F. Hartman, C.SS.R. (Daniel); Joachim Jeremias (Gospel of Luke); George Mendenhall (Laws of the Pentateuch); Johannes Munck (Book of Acts); Jacob M. Myers (Chronicler's history); W.F. Orr and D.N. Freedman (Literature of the New Testament); Marvin H. Pope (Book of Job); Bo Reicke (General Epistles); R.B.Y. Scott (Book of Proverbs); Edward F. Siegman, C.PP.S., (Revelation of John); E.A. Speiser (Book of Genesis); Krister Stendahl (Pauline Epistles, I and II); G. Ernest Wright (Deuteronomic History).

the work provides a foundation for the expectation that the common Bible is actually in the making. Each man on their team has a solid reputation for objective scholarship. Many of them would probably prefer to be known simply as philologists. In this project none of them will have a theological axe to grind. Dr. Albright and Dr. Freedman have arranged with the publisher of the new translation (Doubleday) that introductions and commentaries will stress the archaeological, historical and literary approaches. There will be some religious and theological "descriptions," but not "interpretations," in the commentary. In the translation itself, as well as in the commentary, the scholars know that their every step will be critically scanned by the rest of the scholarly world when the finished work is presented for review by theological and biblical journals. The translation, which will be in idiomatic modern English, will be published in 30 paperback volumes in Doubleday's Anchor Book series.[23]

In the Anchor Bible project, as in all modern scholarly efforts, Catholics and Protestants use the same critical editions of the original languages, the same lexicons, the same archaeological reports. They study the same articles and books for whatever light they can shed on the problems that arise. If their common scholarship results in a joint Bible, it will have restored to the Christian people the common language and common concepts they once had and still need for the achieving of Christian unity. It can be done. After all, as F.F. Bruce has pointed out, "it is, in any case, not so much the wording of the Bible—whether it is or is not in itself the sufficient rule of faith and practice—that keeps Protestants and Roman Catholics apart."[24]

"Things that are impossible with men are possible with God." After quoting this text as a comment on the task of reunifying the divided Christian world, Msgr. John J. Dougherty, biblical scholar and president of Seton Hall University, continued a Chair of Unity Octave sermon in St. Patrick's Cathedral, New York, with a summary of recent events that led him to find interchurch relations at their best since the Protestant

[23]The first volumes are scheduled to appear in 1962, the last in 1966.
[24]F.F. Bruce, *op. cit.*, p. 209.

Reformation.[25] These events, he said, were the friendly contacts between Pope John XXIII and Patriarch Athenagoras of the Orthodox Church, the "courtesy" visit of the retiring Archbishop of Canterbury to the Vatican, the growing dialogue between Protestant and Catholic theologians, and the increasing possibility of a common English translation of the Bible. All these things, Msgr. Dougherty stressed, are manifestations of promise, not of fulfillment. In view of Christ's prayer that all be one, however, we may add that it is surely the Christian thing to hope and pray that these manifestations of promise be fulfilled.

---

[25]The sermon, delivered on January 23, 1961, was reported the next day in *The New York Times*, p. 17.

The Liturgy and Reunion

by Shawn G. Sheehan

The liturgical apostolate originated and developed without explicit reference to the needs of the ecumenical effort. Both movements have been referred to by recent popes as movements prompted by the Holy Spirit. Almost from the beginning it became evident that the liturgical apostolate had a real value in the formation of Catholic ecumenists, that its teachings are important in the actual dialogue and that it helps to create a more favorable atmosphere among the clergy and laity for the advance of Christian reunion. It has also been evident that sincere participation in the liturgy imposes the obligation to work zealously for the reunion of all Christians.

UNION WITH CHRIST IN PRAYER

When we speak of the Church's liturgy we are not speaking principally of the outward forms, of rites and the external aspect of active participation. Nor are we speaking only of the Church's worshipful response to the goodness of God manifested in Christ. We are speaking also and in fact primarily of the Incarnate Son's own worship of the Father and our participation in his worship. This is the meaning of the liturgy given in *Mediator Dei,* where it is defined as "the public worship which our Redeemer as Head of the Church renders to the Father as well as the worship which the community of the faithful renders to its Founder, and through him to the Heavenly Father."

The key is in the understanding of Christ as our Head

and Mediator. Historians have shown how this understanding was obscured in the defense of the faith against denials of Christ's divinity, his real presence in the Blessed Sacrament, the sacrificial character of the Mass, and so on. Every effort had to be made, through preaching, hymns, revisions in liturgical rites, formulation of extra-liturgical devotions, and so on, to impress upon the faithful the true doctrine and to keep them from any infection of error. The necessary ends were achieved and classifications in doctrine were made but there were inevitable disadvantages. The concept of union with Christ our Mediator in the worship of God was obscured, and there followed a decline in active participation in the liturgy. Devotional life was oriented in such a way as to express adherence to the doctrines that were attacked or to satisfy aspirations that were left unsatisfied as active liturgical participation declined.

The piety that was developed did greatly enrich the Church's life and it produced heroic generations and great saints. Moreover, it contains many permanent values and even devotional forms that should never be sacrificed. Under papal leadership a re-orientation is going on now, centered in appreciation of the Headship and Mediation of Christ. In regard to the ecumenical effort there are real advantages. The older forms of piety could by themselves be an obstacle to this effort, for they tend to accentuate our differences from other Christians and to make us poorly disposed to appreciate their piety and aspirations. A sense of dynamic union with Christ in prayer focuses attention more fully on the source and center of unity.

PERSONAL ENCOUNTERS WITH CHRIST

The decline in appreciation of the Church as the Mystical Body of Christ also had an effect on worship, for there was a consequent decline in the realization that the sacraments are acts of Christ, who is always living and acting in his Church. The emphasis was chiefly on Christ's historical institution of the sacraments and on their efficacy "ex opere operato." Such a view can leave many persons with a very superficial piety. The sacraments may seem to be a set of helpful devices for getting grace. The personal relationship with Christ may seem remote. Historians tell us that such a superficial view was common in the late Middle Ages. This is part of the reason why Protestantism was marked from the first by a strong aspiration for personal religion, a vital union with Christ by faith. It is part of the Protestant charge that the Catholic Church, with its priesthood and sacramental system, gets between the soul and God, interposing a set of mechanical devices for achieving holiness.

A reform was needed in the Church. It was already going on and was clearly and effectively directed by the Council of Trent. Many factors, such as the bitterness of doctrinal controversy and the spread of Jansenism, intervened to make the reform less effective than it should have been. During the past half-century a new advance has been made in our appreciation of the sacraments. The encyclicals of Pope Pius XII on the Mystical Body and on the Liturgy have been the chief contributions. In the past few years in this country a profound and far-reaching advance is noticeable, largely under the influence of a talk given by Father Godfrey Diekmann of St. John's Abbey at the 1957 Liturgical Week and published both in *Worship* (Oct. 1957) and in the *Proceedings* of the Week (*Education and the Liturgy*). This talk, entitled "Two Approaches to Understanding the Sacraments,"[1] brings out the importance of the sacramental signs for arousing faith and eliciting personal response, and it shows the way in which St. Thomas gave an integral presentation of the sacraments by giving both signification and causality their due importance.

FORMATION BY WORD OF GOD

The liturgical restoration has been closely allied with some of the recent developments in Biblical theology and catechetics. There is a new appreciation of the continuity of the works of God from generation to generation, in creation, in the covenant with the chosen people of old, in the redemption by Christ and in the Church.

[1]Reprinted in *Come, Let Us Worship* (Baltimore, Helicon Press, 1961), pp. 23–40.

The opening talk in the Liturgical Week on liturgy and unity in 1960, "God's Call to Worship," brought out the fact that the Church has been formed by God's Word and its worship is a response to God. The Church did not come into being as an association of those who are willing to believe certain doctrines and obey certain rules. Neither was it created to serve utilitarian ends such as peace of mind or a better social order. Christian unity is not to be sought ultimately through agreements among the various groups professing faith in Christ. The Church is a divine creation. In the establishment of the Church by Christ, God has called men to unity and to worship.

In presenting the meaning of the liturgy today writers in the liturgical apostolate, on both the popular and scholarly levels, generally start with the Church, the assembly of the people called by God. Not only is this good pedagogy, giving the faithful a sense of involvement right from the start, but it makes clear the principle that Christian sanctification and worship follow from God's call and that this takes place primarily in the community. Through participation in the liturgy we also affirm and we deepen our realization of both the visible nature of the Church and the personal union with God in the Church.

Scripture scholars are showing the close tie between the Biblical transmission of God's word and the liturgical assemblies in both the Old Testament period and the apostolic age. There is also developing today a better appreciation of the efficacy of the proclamation of God's word in a liturgical gathering.

We turn also to the Scriptures to find the form of our response to God, a response to be made by minds and hearts formed by God's word and expressing themselves in inspired prayers, prayers offered now with Christ, our Mediator with God.

In recovering the importance of the signification of the sacraments we turn to the Old Testament for the preparations and types, to the New Testament for the actions of Christ and the themes in his teaching that explain their meaning and efficacy, and to the sacramental rites developed by the Church for the readings, allusions and prayers, generally Biblical, that arouse our faith and elicit the proper response.

THE EUCHARIST, SACRAMENT OF UNITY

One of the principal efforts in the liturgical apostolate has been to restore to the consciousness of clergy and laity the mystery so often emphasized by Pope Pius XII, for example in his encyclical on the Mystical Body, in which he said, "Through the Eucharistic Sacrifice Christ our Lord wished to give special evidence to the faithful of our union among ourselves and with our divine Head," and also, "in the Holy Eucharist the faithful are nourished and grow strong at the same table, and in a divine, ineffable way are brought into union with each other and with the divine Head of the whole Body."

The celebration of the Holy Sacrifice is not just an action which the priest performs at the altar in virtue of powers handed down from Christ and the apostles through the ages. The laity do not merely attend, expressing their belief, adoration, thanks and petition. Christ himself is present uniting all, both priest and laity, with himself. The celebrant presides and exercises distinctive powers but all are united with each other and with Christ in offering his Sacrifice. All are co-victims and co-offerers with Christ and they offer themselves not only as individuals but as a community, becoming perfected together as an offering to God in Christ. This action engages each one in an intimate, vital personal union with Christ. It is obvious that to prepare the laity for fully sincere participation the clergy must give them instruction and spiritual formation not only in the liturgy as such but also in daily living dominated by charity and its relation to worship.

Moreover, in the Eucharistic Sacrifice we are invited to God's table. "Because the bread is one, we though many, are one body, all of us who partake of the one bread."

ECUMENICAL FORMATION

Intelligent participation in the liturgy gives us a better realization of Christ's active presence in the Church and from this comes a better understanding of the Church's unity: that is, that the Church is not merely an organization which continues

Christ's teaching, promulgates divine law for each generation, worships God as Christ instructed and dispenses his grace, but that it is all this and more, that it is a living organism, Christ's Mystical Body, in which he himself is doing these things. Moreover, with a consciousness of this living unity, we should become more deeply concerned about the existence of disunity among Christians, we should enter more sympathetically into the dialogue with those who feel with us the scandal of disunity, and we should be better instruments of Christ in the effort for unity.

In the formation of a right attitude to other Christians (and to non-Christians) the liturgical outlook helps us to be free of smug partisanship and helps us to see ourselves as instruments of Christ, approaching others with an attitude as close as possible to that of the Savior himself. There seems to be a tendency on the part of many to see the situation in the following terms. They think of Christ in Heaven; they think of themselves as his faithful followers here on earth, and they think of others as his enemies. So out of loyalty to Christ they carry on a campaign that consists largely of convincing others how right we are and how wrong they are. They seek to win others over to their allegiance to Christ's teaching. It would be better to see Christ living in his Church, living in us, using us as his instruments, through us coming into contact with others and doing so in the ways characteristic of his redemptive work, which does indeed include patient teaching and correction of error, but is accomplished chiefly by love and sacrifice. There is, moreover, the fact that we carry on the Christian dialogue with persons who are Christians, baptized, united with Christ, believers in him and devoted to him. They lack full membership in the Church but they are heirs of unfortunate splits within Christendom itself.

We are instruments of Christ, the Good Shepherd, who brings together his sheep into one fold. He has laid down his life for his sheep. He has said to us, "Learn of me, for I am meek and humble of heart."

Many Orthodox and Protestants are vitally concerned with many of the aspects of the Christian life that we have been considering, and many of these considerations have contributed toward their zeal for the ecumenical movement. Experience shows that these matters are of real importance in ecumenical dialogue.

Ecclesiology and Ecumenics

by Gustave Weigel, S.J.

Broad, devastating generalizations can seem to be over-simplifications. But to use generalizations is not a defect, even though some people think so. As long as I do not use universalizations, my position is modest.

First of all, I would like to point out that I shall not address myself to the subject given. Permit me to make a slight modification. I do not wish to deal with Ecclesiology and Reunion. I wish to discuss ecclesiology and ecumenics. Ecumenics and reunion are different concepts. In ecumenics, the purpose of endeavor is not the union of the churches. The purpose of the endeavor is to bring together separate Churches to whatever degree is possible at a given moment. No ecumenist who believes in God, Christ, and the Church thinks that it can be a human purpose to make one Church of the many. Only God can do this, and that is why prayer is necessary in the ecumenical effort. Men can do something, and their purpose is to bring the Churches together so that they will meet in friendship and hold dialogues of clarification. It is hoped, and a high hope it is, that such conversation will be an occasion which the Spirit will use to bring the Churches out of division to the Unity desired by Christ.

Ecclesiology, when I studied it as a student, was called *de ecclesia.* Today it has become quite common to call the same treatise ecclesiology. This change of title was not intended to be highly significant, but I do think that it did show the intention of presenting *de ecclesia* from a different point of view.

Modern ecclesiology within the Catholic Church has taken on a coloring which was absent in the old *de ecclesia* tract. Why is this so? I think there were three different movements which pressed on the ecclesiologists to construct their treatise in a different way.

The first movement was the ecumenical movement. It is inevitable that ecumenism will raise the question of Church. Its hope is a united Church. Its most conspicuous product in our time is the World Council of Churches. The word "church" stands out so boldly that, necessarily, theologians—Catholic, Protestant and Orthodox—had to face the question of the precise meaning of the church.

The second influence, namely, the biblical revival has already been considered. By reason of the new approach to Scripture and the seriousness of Scripture studies within the Church, it was necessary for ecclesiologists to go back to the Scriptures in a new way and, in my opinion, in a far more solid way.

The third influence must not be overlooked, although it is not directly theological. It is the liturgical movement: the life of the Church, as expressed in common worship. Liturgy necessarily raised the question of Church as matrix for the life of prayer. Therefore, these three movements, ecumenical, biblical and liturgical produced developments in Catholic ecclesiology.

What do we find as a result of these developments? The first note is that the Church is a mystery; that the Church is something in which I believe: *"credo ecclesiam catholicam,"* that it is not the object of sheerly phenomenal investigation. An historian, who will report to me as accurately as an historian can the events of the life of the Church for two thousand years cannot even touch the Church, because the Church is something to be achieved in faith. It is something God-given. It can only be understood in terms of her own life and in terms of her own vision.

This brought about a change within Catholic ecclesiology. Today, the apologetic approach, the so-called historical-philosophical method, is being abandoned more and more. The treatise on the Church is a dogmatic treatise. The truth of the Church is derived from God's revelation communicated to us by the Church.

Ecclesiologists are doing theology. We do not attempt historical work ending in conclusions far beyond the merit of the premises. By revelation, by Catholic light and commitment, we understand the Church. This is rather important. Because it is a dogmatic treatise, it is necessary for us to use all the sources of revelation at the disposal of the theologian.

Of all the sources, highest in dignity and most universal in appeal will be the Scriptures. Therefore, the modern ecclesiologist goes back to the Scripture in a way which was usual, let us say, before 1930. We all know that all theology within the Catholic tradition is always heavily scriptural, but fifty years ago too much was added to the Scripture and the Scripture itself was taken out of its context and given explanations which were no longer truly biblical.

I remember very well that when I was taught *de ecclesia,* we did all kinds of proving from the notion of Kingdom of God. But no one at my time, in my place, bothered to understand and investigate what *βασιλεία τοῦ θεοῦ* meant in the Scripture. We were told it meant the power of governing, expressed completely and succinctly in terms of the executive power, the legislative power and the judicial power, and this was the meaning of *βασιλεία τοῦ θεοῦ.*

No one then mentioned that this understanding of government was taken from Montesquieu and not from Matthew. Therefore, we now go back to the Scriptural symbols. There are almost a hundred of such symbols in the New Testament explaining the Church, but there are for our purposes especially four: *Q'āhāl* translated in Greek as *ekklesia.* This term cannot be taken as something already known. We must find out what the *Q'āhāl ecclesia* correspondence meant in the Scripture. Secondly, great value is given today, as perhaps never before, to the Church under the symbolic explanation of the *σῶμα τοῦ χριστοῦ,* the "Mystical Body." Today in all theologates this symbol plays a large part in explaining the Church as Life and as Mystery. We have dropped, in consequence, the heavily juridical presentation of the Church. The older *de ecclesia* treatise fell into the danger of describing the Church merely as government. She was mainly conceived in terms of law. This is no longer true. In fact, I would say the modern ecclesiologist is almost embarrassed by the fact that there *is* a genuinely legal and juridical element in the Church. He finds this side somewhat uncongenial to his interest. There is here a danger in modern ecclesiology, but at least in facing this danger it avoids the juridicism which marks so much of *de ecclesia* treatment in the past.

The Protestants have their own ecclesiology and it is interesting to see how they have come forward.

Calvin made a great deal of the fact that the Church, the Church praised and highly regarded in the Scriptures, was an invisible Church. He says in his preface to the Institutes, "You always ask me, *digito indicare,* to point out the Church with a finger."

Calvin denied that this could be done. For him the Church was the sum total of men who had in faith committed themselves to Christ. In our time some Protestant ecumenists put the matter this way: *ubi Christus ibi Ecclesia.* The stress, therefore, is not on the visible side of the Church. The Church is primarily the inner realm of God. Yet contemporary Protestants want more than an invisible Church. Now, they appreciate and state forthrightly that the Church is in fact also visible and must be visible.

Protestants no longer consider it a good definition of the Church to say she is a congregation of like-minded men. That is not enough. They also insist that it is not merely a question of meeting where the Gospel is genuinely preached and the Sacraments genuinely administered. They realize that this would cut off the congregation from that large ecumenical reality which is the Church.

As a result of this ecumenical conception of Church there has been a new Protestant interest in tradition. In the light of what has been said just before, let me point out what the brilliant Lutheran theologian, Jaroslav Pelikan, is frequently saying. For him tradition is first of all primitive. Before the written word there is the tradition. Secondly, tradition is inevitable. To use the words of the Orthodox theologian, Father George Florovsky, who is also working in this field, the choice is not between tradition and no tradition; the choice is between good tradition and bad tradition. The last point of Jaroslav Pelikan is that tradition is necessarily exegetical.

Now, this shows a movement within Protestant ecclesiology and it is very significant. Protestant theologians want a unity in ecumenical approach in the light of a tradition which can be recognized as valid and the true voice of the ecumenical Church.

You will notice that on both sides, Protestant and Catholic, there has been a convergence. Catholics are now stressing the mystery of the Church. They present the Church as Life. Now, this is in line with the old Protestant notion of the Invisible Church. We overcome the danger of onesidedness by insisting that there is only one Church. She is both visible and invisible and she is truly one. However, we are constructing a notion of Church as a vitality which is Divine life.

On the part of the Protestants the movement is toward an element dear to Catholics, the necessity of tradition; the necessity of an ecumenical Church, a Church which is not merely invisible but is necessarily visible as well. We are pursuing converging lines of thought—not identical, but truly converging.

When will they meet? I am neither a prophet nor the son of a prophet. I refuse to answer the question.

Now, ecclesiology is expressly and explicitly an ecumenical concern, and we have here a difficulty. The World Council of Churches does not and cannot profess an ecclesiology and yet an ecclesiology is active in the World Council. The dynamic secretary of the World Council of Churches, Dr. Willem Visser 't Hooft tells us that there are indeed ecclesiological postulates working in the World Council, but no formal ecclesiology.

I am perfectly willing to recognize the validity of his observation, but the postulate is that every Church within the Council already is in the Church of Christ. Now, this particular postulate offers difficulties.

The Orthodox must handle it as best they can. It is interesting, as Father Boyer's paper points out, that there is progress on the Catholic side.

Yes, indeed, we must hold that the Holy Roman Catholic

Church is the Mystical Body of Christ. There is no more Catholicism outside of the Mystical Body than there is outside of the Roman Catholic Church. They are identical. Yet, when faced with this question of churches which are not Roman Catholic, the present-day ecclesiologists must move onward. To me it was highly consoling to see that for Father Boyer, as for me, the basis of our thinking must be *extra ecclesiam nulla salus.* I think this decides the question ultimately. But there are questions to be resolved.

For example, the point is sometimes raised that we have an expression in Pope Pius XII's encyclical where he says the Church, over and above its juridic bonds which it has in common with other societies, has another principle of unity which is the Holy Spirit, so that the Church is a *corpus animatum.*

On that principle, according to St. Augustine, if a body withdraws from the Church as a limb is severed from the body, the soul does not follow the severed member. So, therefore, the resulting society could not be deserving of the name Church, except by way of analogy, or courtesy, or a *figura ecclesiae.* It is not actually an *ecclesia* in a theological sense.

I believe that we can give a perfectly adequate answer to this objection. It is a Church *per modum analogiae,* where the *analogatum primarium* is the Roman Catholic Church which is the Mystical Body of Christ. Analogically this other church can truly be called a Church, but I would merely insist that this analogy is intrinsic and ontological. Consequently, it is not at all surprising that some of the treasures which God gave to his Church can be found in these other communities. They have baptism, they have the Scriptures, they have the Christian tradition—imperfectly, if you will, but they have them. It is untrue to say that Christ is totally absent from their meetings. There is some sense, good sense, in the phrase which they like to use: *ubi Christus ibi ecclesia.*

It will be necessary to think through all of this patiently and thoroughly. We can expect a good number of studies and articles on membership in the Church; the difference between those who are members and those who belong to or pertain to the Church in some way; on the degree of their belongingness; or in whatever way they pertain to it.

Many feel that the difference between those in the Church and those outside rests on the presence or absence of baptism. Yet, not all baptized believers are equally attached to the Church.

Another aspect of the problem might be stated in the terms of Father Gregory Baum's book, *That They May Be One* (Westminster, Newman, 1958). In it he also treats of the analogous predication of the Church, yet he seems to speak of Protestants as imperfect members of the Church. But the distinction that I have made is different. There are *formal* members of the Church, and they are those who are baptized and who are recognized by the law of the Church.

There are two classes of these: those who are perfect members because they are in the state of grace; those who are imperfect members because they are not in the state of grace.

What is the double thing which makes me a Catholic? My baptismal character and the recognition by the Church through her law that I am a member. Now, take those who are baptized and are excommunicated by our law. They have baptism. They haven't got recognition. They have, therefore, the *radix membreitatis*, the *character baptismalis* which they have forever and indelibly. They do not have the *forma membreitatis*. But they are radical members.

Then there are the virtual members, whether they have *character baptismalis* or not, if they have been justified by God by uncovenanted mercy in a manner extraordinary because God is the lover of souls. These men, by an act of faith, grace-given by the Lord, and by an act of charity, grace-given by the Lord, are in sanctifying Grace, which is the property of the Church. Having the property of the Church they are as if they were members. These I call virtual members.

The Church is one. Where there are many churches, only one is formally that Church—but the others somehow adhere to it. What does the ecclesiologist have to do in the face of this paradox? He must work hard with sweat and patience, to find a definition which will clarify the issue. In this task ecclesiology is now engaged.

Eastern Churches and Primacy

by Paul Mailleux, S.J.

A few weeks after the announcement of the new Ecumenical Council Father George Florovsky, the well-known Russian theologian, wrote an article on that event in a Russian Orthodox magazine and drew the following conclusion: "At the present time the Orthodox have as their first duty the obligation to ask themselves a fundamental question and to study it for themselves in all its tragic complications: What happened in 1054—or perhaps even earlier, or perhaps only later? In what does the essence of the Schism consist? What exactly is the 'Roman Church' from the viewpoint of Orthodox Ecclesiology? Did the Roman Church, and to what extent did she, keep 'Orthodoxy'—I mean the true faith—or did she hopelessly fall into heresy? We must begin precisely with that." Father Florovsky writes further, "It is obvious that among the Orthodox there is no uniform teaching about these points, and we should put that question very sincerely and openly."

These lines by one of the leading Orthodox writers are in striking contrast to the attitudes of the Orthodox Patriarchs when they were invited by Pius IX to the Vatican Council ninety years ago. At that time the Orthodox world simply rejected the invitation of the Church of Rome. This time Father Florovsky and other Orthodox writers with him at least invite their co-religionists to some reflection. "Before anything else," writes Father Florovsky in his conclusion, "we must study and explain our doctrine on the Church in all its fulness and complexity."[1]

[1]"About the Coming Roman Council," *The Messenger of Orthodox Students* (*Viestnik,* in Russian), January 1959, p. 5.

This new attitude toward the Church of Rome is no doubt a consequence of the new situation in which the Eastern Christians not united with Rome have been finding themselves since the end of Turkish domination in the Near East and, more particularly, since the Russian Revolution in 1917.

The Old Roman Empire of the East, the Byzantine Empire, existed for more than eleven centuries. During that exceptionally long existence it was a real theocracy which always knew —at least in theory—a remarkable union of Church and State. Between the two there reigned a so-called "symphony." The Church was an imperial Church and the Empire wanted to be truly Christian. Considering himself the legate on earth of the Heavenly Sovereign, the Emperor took upon himself the responsibility not only to worship God in the name of his people, but also to make thorough provision for both the spiritual as well as the temporal welfare of his subjects. That Byzantine concept of Church-State relations was carried to the nations which received Christianity through Byzantium. It prevailed for about nine hundred years at the courts of the three successive capitals of Russia: Kiev, Moscow and Saint Petersburg.

But the nineteenth and still more the twentieth century abruptly placed most of the Eastern Christian communities in new conditions of life. Instead of protecting the Church, the Soviet State tried to suffocate her. So also did the Communist governments of the smaller states (Serbia, Bulgaria and Rumania) which had freed themselves a few decades earlier from Turkish domination.

In the same period millions of Orthodox left their native countries of the East to establish themselves in Western Europe, in America or in Australia. There are now probably about three million Orthodox in the United States alone. Therefore, the so-called "Eastern Churches" are not exclusively Eastern any more. Their faithful are spread throughout the West and, even in the East, they are facing the same religious problems as the Western Church. Some of these communities of Orthodox emigrants try to remain under the jurisdiction of their former hierarchs in the Old World. Some have created independent hierarchies. Some others have placed themselves again under obedience to the Patriarch of Constantinople. Finally, some others—mostly the younger generations in the United States—ask insistently for the creation of an American Autocephalous Church, for an American Orthodox Patriarchate (which would unite the twenty Orthodox groups spread over the country). They also want every group to use English as the common liturgical language.

Sometimes bitter conflicts have arisen among them, originating not only from ethnical opposition but also from different political outlooks. Therefore, the most crucial question for them, since their communities are separated from the State, seems to be the establishment of a new basis: a fundamental principle for what they call their *constitutional right.* In front of them stands the monolithic, as they often call her, Roman Catholic Church, which claims as the basis for her constitutional right nothing less than a divine institution. Slowly, more thoughtful Orthodox theologians have begun to reconsider their old attitude towards the Roman Church, and even to look for some kind of reconciliation and collaboration with her.

Mr. Anton Kartashoff (who died in Paris on September 10, 1960) was the first well-known Orthodox writer to try to establish a constructive project for a reconciliation with Rome, (we should say more exactly, for a peaceful coexistence). He had been the last Procurator of the Holy Synod under the last Tzar, Minister of Ecclesiastical Affairs under Kerensky and, in the emigration, professor of Church History at the Orthodox Seminary in Paris.

He expressed his thoughts in an article written in Russian for a symposium on Christian Reunion.[2] In his concluding remarks he explains that reunion is possible only if each Christian community does penance for its past errors: "For what must Protestants do penance? Evidently, for having rejected the hierarchical gift of the Holy Spirit and, with that gift, a great part of the other sacraments and some ancient apostolic traditions such as the veneration of the Saints.

[2]"Christian Reunion," *The Ecumenical Problem in the Orthodox Conscience* (in Russian) (Paris, YMCA Press, no date), p. 82.

"For what must the Roman Catholics do penance? For having held in contempt the obligation of universal charity in the Church and the prescriptions of the ecumenical councils—by their own authority changing the symbol of the faith. They broke away from that union of love and created for themselves the dogma of the Papacy, which has become the obstacle to the ecumenical union of the Churches."

But the author's judgment on the Orthodox Church is more unexpected. "For what must the Orthodox do penance? For the fact that they too, by lack of a total and universal love for the Church, ceased to be attentive to the theology of the West at a time when the West (openly and in good faith) was elaborating and developing its dogmas of the *Filioque* and papal power. The Orientals, concerned only with the welfare of the Imperial Church, did not object in time to the growing mystique of the papal dogma; they subscribed in silence to the pronouncements of Pope Leo the Great, Adrian I and many others.

"With their irresponsible juridical appeals to Rome, with their 'Romophily' (as for example, that of Saint Theodore the Studite), they developed amongst the Latins an illusion that the Greeks also shared their Western way of understanding the mystique of the Primacy. Pope Nicholas I with sincerity called the Primacy a 'Sacrament' and the Greeks with levity—yes, with levity—even at the Council of Florence, thought that the matter was only administrative priority or ambition. Because of their neglect of western spirituality and their ignorance of it, the Greeks are guilty of having contributed to the strengthening of the *Filioque* and more specially of the Papacy. They began only at a very late date to refute these dogmas, thus creating the impression in the western world that the Greeks were false traitors who at first expressed no objections and then later refused to agree. In reality, of course, this is not true, but the Greeks are responsible for the creation of such a misunderstanding." So for Mr. Kartashoff the evil is done. A way of reconciliation must be found. Here is his proposal: "If the Roman Catholics wish to re-establish the ancient ecclesiastic communion in love with the East, they must renounce only one thing: the 'universalism' of papal power, not that power itself. And the Orthodox Church must recognize all their new dogmas as 'theologoumena'. The Roman Papacy is so deeply and organically united to the structure, history, life and piety of the Latin Church, that to demand its suppression would be in her eyes equal to perpetrating an attack on the whole mystique of Latin Church piety. To us Orientals such an attempt seems simply like the old Protestant impious bitterness. We must understand the piety of the Roman Catholic, his ecclesiological mystique, which personifies the heart of the Church in the Pope. Whose violent hand would attempt to tear out the heart of our Western brethren, that delicate flower which has grown out of their love for the Church?

"The Orthodox," writes Mr. Kartashoff finally, "must admit the Pope for the Roman Church, not only as the first in honor among the autocephalous patriarchs (this is elementary), but as a mystical pope for the Latins. They must see the papacy as a special monarchical organ of ecclesiastical infallibility, according to their Latin faith, which stands above the councils. But all this would be held only within the limits of the Roman Patriarchate—even if it extends over the whole earthly sphere—as long as it does not absorb in itself all the Churches. We understand very well," he confesses, "that for the Roman Catholic a Papacy limited not in its qualitative meaning but in its quantitative extension is nonsense. But what can we do? One must be able to renounce one's customary way of thinking for the sake of the truth and of the ecumenical unity of the Church."

Precisely for the sake of the truth Mr. Kartashoff's proposal was unacceptable to Catholics. But his article was not useless. It recalled to the attention of many Orthodox how often even the Greek Fathers had professed the Roman primacy.

Another professor of the Russian seminary in Paris, Father Nicholas Afanasieff, presented new considerations on the same subject in a book published in Russian six years ago under the title of *The Lord's Table.*[3] Since that time he has again outlined his ideas in several articles. On the same subject he wrote

---

[3]N. Afanasieff, *The Lord's Table* (in Russian) (Paris, 1955). See also *Istina,* 1957, No. 4.

very recently one of the four articles published in a symposium in French on "La Primauté de Pierre dans l'Eglise Orthodoxe" (The Primacy of Peter in the Orthodox Church).[4]

According to Father Afanasieff there are two conceptions of the Church. He calls them *eucharistic ecclesiology* and *universal ecclesiology*. In the early period of the Church, he claims, Christians lived in the spirit of eucharistic ecclesiology. At that time nobody thought of the universality of the Church. The Church which all had in mind was the local Church. Between that Church and the Eucharist there was such an intimate connection that they had a common name. Both were called "the Body of Christ."

"Each Church was autonomous, because," as Father Afanasieff writes, "the Church of God in Christ possesses the fulness of existence outside of which nothing exists because outside of Christ nothing can exist. One cannot apply to the Church," he writes further, "the arithmetic of Euclid, because in ecclesiology we operate on quantities which one can not add up. The plurality of local Churches does not destroy the unity of the Church of God as the plurality of eucharistic assemblies does not destroy the unity of the Eucharist in time and space."

In the first centuries all Churches were equal. This does not mean that there were no relations among them. On the contrary, brotherly relations among them meant only that they accepted and admitted the faith of the other and the conformity of their behavior to the Will of God.

Among these churches there was no *primacy* which would involve a power of one of them over the other, but a *priority* or a kind of seniority without juridical authority. At the earliest stage, that *priority* belonged to the Church of Jerusalem. From there it was transferred to Rome. Father Afanasieff sees in the letters of Saint Clement, Saint Ignatius of Antioch, Saint Ireneus of Lyon, a recognition of that priority. Saint Ignatius describes perfectly the exact position of the Church of Rome when he calls her *"the Church which presides in love."*

The other conception of the Church, that of universal ecclesiology, appeared at the time of Saint Cyprian and probably

[4]Published in Switzerland (Neuchatel: Delachaux & Niestle, 1960).

took its inspiration from the structure of the Roman Empire, in which the world was juridically unified under the guidance of the Emperor. Once somebody agrees to that universal ecclesiology, he must logically admit also a primacy in the Church, be it the primacy of the Pope for the Church of Rome or the primacy of Metropolitans in the autocephalous Orthodox Churches.

Obviously, for Father Afanasieff, universal ecclesiology was a deviation. It has led to the division of Christendom and the problem of reunion. Therefore that problem is, in fact, a problem resulting from false suppositions.

A serious analysis of Father Afanasieff's thesis could fill a volume. It would require, in particular, an exegesis of his quotations from the New Testament and from the Apostolic Fathers. The constructive part of his articles in which he reminds us that the primary foundation of ecclesiastical unity is eucharistic communion, is most felicitous and inspiring. The jurisdiction of the hierarchy, the loyalty of the faithful to their pastors —all that one can call its exterior organization—are essential in the Church but they are not an end in themselves. They are only the means and conditions for carrying into effect the primary mission of the Church, the union of all with Christ: that union which is symbolized and effected in the Eucharist—"*Eucharistia facit Ecclesiam*" (the Eucharist makes the Church).

It was normal and even providential, therefore, that the Christians of the early centuries built a eucharistic ecclesiology before stressing the juridical aspect of the relation of Christian communities among themselves. But it is impossible to follow Father Afanasieff when he considers universal ecclesiology as a deviation. The main reason, though not the only one, is the following: Fr. Afanasieff readily admits that since Saint Cyprian universal ecclesiology has become by far the common ecclesiology of the Church in the East as in the West. If it were a deviation, would we not be obliged to admit that Christ deprived his Church, at a very early period of her existence and in an essential matter, of that assistance which he had promised her? Therefore, another leading Orthodox theologian, Father Alexander Schmemann, in an article published in English, French and Russian, has further developed Father Afanasieff's considerations on eucharistic ecclesiology. But he does not seem to consider any longer that universal ecclesiology is a deviation. "In the present canonical structure of the Church," he writes, "*supreme power* not only exists but it is commonly conceived as the foundation of the Church and as the basis of its canonical system. Such supreme ecclesiastical government is always characterized as power over bishops who are therefore subordinated to it. Supreme power is thus introduced into the very structure of the Church as its essential element."[5]

"In the light of this doctrine," he writes, "the use for and the reality of a visible head (that is, the bishop of Rome) can no longer be termed an exaggeration. It becomes not only acceptable but necessary. If the Church is a universal organism, she must have at her head a universal bishop as the focus of her Unity and the organ of supreme power. The idea, popular in Orthodox apologetics, that the Church can have no visible head, because Christ is her *invisible* head, is theological nonsense. If applied consistently, it should also eliminate the necessity of the visible head of each local church—that is, the bishop. Yet it is the basic assumption of a 'Catholic' ecclesiology that the visible structure of the Church manifests and communicates its invisible nature.

"An objective study of canonical tradition cannot fail to establish beyond any doubt that along with local centers of agreement or primacies the Church has also known a universal primacy." Where is then, the error of Rome? "The error lies in the identification of this primacy with *supreme power* which transforms Rome into the "*Principium, radix et origo*" of the Unity of the Church and of the Church herself.[6] This ecclesiological distortion, however, must not force us into a simple rejection of universal primacy. On the contrary, it ought to encourage its genuinely Orthodox interpretation."

---

[5]"The Idea of Primacy in Orthodox Ecclesiology," *Saint Vladimir's Seminary Quarterly,* vol. 4 (New York, 1960), p. 49.

[6]These words are taken from the letter sent by the Holy Office in 1864 to the English Bishops to reject the Branch Theory. In that letter, the supreme authority of Peter and his successors is called "*principium, radix et origo*" of the *unity* of the Church, not of the Church herself.

Perhaps a few clarifications on the genuine Catholic interpretation of the Primacy would help our Orthodox friends realize that, in point of fact, between their interpretation and ours there is not the opposition which they fear.[7]

The considerations expressed throughout Father Schmemann's article help us to understand better what seems to him unacceptable in the *supreme power.* Fr. Schmemann refuses to admit an authority which would be extrinsic to the Church, dominating the Church from the outside—an authority to which the Church would be subjected as the employees in a big shop are subjected to the owner of the shop (or even more, as slaves are subjected to their master). Such an interpretation, however, is completely foreign to the genuine Catholic doctrine. The successor of Peter is the Supreme Pastor *in* the Church, not *over* the Church as if he were ruling from outside of the Church. Very happily spiritual writers have often seen the Church foreshadowed in the fishing-boat of Peter. In his boat Peter was not at all a captain standing in the middle of slave-rowers and cracking his whip to have them row more vigorously. He was sitting *among* the others, rowing *with* the others, *as* the others. But he was also the one who would take the initiative and say to the others, "Let us go fishing," and would coordinate their rowing. He was not imposing his orders on the others as the whim took him but was acting for the general welfare of the crew.

The power in the Catholic Church can be called monarchical, this is true. But in point of fact, the constitutional right of the Church cannot adequately be compared to that of any monarchy of this world. The Church is not a limited monarchy in which the king receives his power from his people nor is it an autocratic monarchy in which the king may say as Louis XIV said, "L'état c'est moi!" If we wish to understand correctly the place and function of the papacy in the Church, we must renounce comparisons with earthly political institutions and consider it in the light of Saint Paul's teaching on the Mystical Body of Christ.

---

[7]See O. Rousseau, O.S.B., "La vraie valeur de l'Episcopat dans l'Eglise," in *Irenicon,* vol. 29 (1956), p. 121.

The bishop of Rome is the visible head of the Church, the ambassador or vicar of Christ who is the Invisible Head of the Church. In a human being the head does not live, does not operate, does not think nor command outside of the structure of the human body. As the Fathers of the Vatican Council noticed, it is the whole body which carries the head. Without the body the head would lose its proper life. A man thinks, in fact, with all his body, but this does not mean that in the structure of a human being the different parts are interchangeable. Each part has a specific and providential role to play.

We say "providential"—this means that each part has been created by God for the well-being, the harmonious growth and the prosperity of the whole. The Church is the Sacrament through which Christ extends in time and space his physical and historical presence among us. That Sacrament was instituted in a gesture of love and only in the light of that love can we understand and grasp the real meaning and extension of Christ's institutions. In other words, Christ has given to Peter and his successors all the authority which is necessary to fulfill their mission of maintaining the unity of the Church and her independence from the State. At the same time Christ has given to the other members of his Mystical Body the power and the liberty of action which they need to fulfill their particular tasks. Whatever our Orthodox friends may fear, even after the Vatican Council the bishops keep their personal authority and responsibility. A letter of the German bishops (approved by Pope Pius IX after the Council) explained it clearly and in detail. Episcopal jurisdiction is not at all absorbed by papal jurisdiction. Therefore, the Pope is not the Archbishop of New York, and the Archbishop of New York is not the Vicar General of the Pope for the New York Archdiocese. The bishops have been instituted by the Holy Spirit and put in the place of the apostles to shepherd and rule in the capacity of true pastors the folds which have been particularly committed to them, and to rule *in solidum* the whole fold (Vatican Council, 3).

Since the announcement of an Ecumenical Council it has very often been written in theological publications that the next Council would enunciate some clarifications on the episcopacy which the Council of 1870, abruptly interrupted by international conflicts, had no time to formulate. Often our Orthodox friends ask us what these clarifications will be. Some are also anxious to know whether the next Council will proclaim a new interpretation of the Pope's infallibility *ex sese et non ex consensu Ecclesiae* which would be, as they say, "less unacceptable to the Orthodox." Of course, nobody can say for sure what the Second Vatican Council will discuss or decide. But anyone who has grasped the fundamental tendency of Catholic ecclesiology knows in advance that, if definitions are proclaimed in that field, they will stress that the Supreme Pastor in the Church has been established by Christ not to exercise a domination over her (which some Orthodox seem to fear) but to serve her. The Papacy is nothing else but a "διακονία," a true service. The title which the Popes use for themselves when they write their official letters, *Servus Servorum Dei*, "Servant of God's servants," is an indication of this tendency.

The same assurance can be given to our Orthodox brethren concerning the solemn definitions of the Pope as irreformable of themselves and not only when the Church expresses approval, *ex sese et non ex consensu Ecclesiae.* Papal infallibility also is nothing else but a "διακονία," a service. It is not given to the Pope to impose on other minds his personal opinion. The Pope will never make definitions *ex cathedra* against or outside the tradition of the Church, or in opposition to the episcopal body. If to proclaim a truth to be believed (*de fide*) the Pope had previously to make sure that he has or will have the approval of the whole Church (*consensus ecclesiae*) he would find himself faced with a practically impossible task. In times of crisis and difficulties the Church would suffer from that situation as she would be deprived of an effective guide. We may well suspect that the Pope would never receive the unanimous approval of all baptized Christians. But what proportion of the faithful would constitute the agreement of the Church (*consensus ecclesiae*) remains an open question. Do the Orthodox not face the same difficulty when they want to establish a criterion of the ecumenicity of a Council? Many Christians refused to accept the decisions of the Council of Chalcedon and, nevertheless, the Orthodox consider it ecumenical. Many Christians—probably the absolute majority—have considered the Council of Florence ecumenical, and still the Orthodox reject it. To help us know the truth with full assurance Christ, in a gesture of love for his Church, protects his ambassador on earth against error when he speaks solemnly and formally in his place.

Unfortunately Father Schmemann's approach to Catholic doctrine is not yet followed by most of the Orthodox writers. Studies published by other Orthodox theologians in the same volumes as his articles still show many prejudices and sometimes a surprising ignorance of the true Catholic teaching. Since the convocation of the Council old anti-Catholic writings have been reprinted and distributed in Orthodox circles. We also should not forget that the primacy of the Bishop of Rome is not the only theological question about which the Orthodox disagree with us. Our doctrines on the Procession of the Holy Spirit, the Immaculate Conception of Mary and the indissolubility of marriage, for example, still raise much opposition among them.

Nevertheless, the articles of Mr. Kartashoff, of Father Afanasieff and Father Schmemann and many others are parts of a peaceful, a serious and a fruitful dialogue which is taking place between our two separated Christian communities. The desire for reconciliation in truth and charity is growing on both sides. The most burning question is obviously always the government of the Church. Therefore, our most urgent duty toward the Eastern Christians not united with us will always be to help them understand that the primacy of the bishop of Rome, which they consider as a yoke to take upon their shoulders, is on the contrary an exalting mystery, a gesture of love proceeding from Christ who wanted to complete the visible and social structure of his Church.

Current Trends in Catholic Ecumenism

by Charles Boyer, S.J.

There are different trends in Catholic ecumenism, and not everybody follows the one I do. If I should present them all and refrain from making judgment (if that were possible) it would not be a very useful thing. But should I indicate a preference, even if I were to justify it—especially, perhaps, if I were to justify it—I would risk giving some displeasure to colleagues of mine in the same great cause of Christian unity. Even so, it seemed to me that in this case of differing points of view it would be the better part to face them in a brotherly way, so as to let the best one win out, or so as to piece together the good that each of them holds.

There thus remained merely the manner of procedure.

One way of treating the subject of the present trends of Catholic ecumenism would be to analyze the rather numerous books which deal with this matter and to study the organizations whose purpose is ecumenical action. I am afraid that this method would be quite long and would risk running into confusion and repetitions. I have found it preferable to distinguish the principal questions entailed in ecumenism, and to seek the different solutions proposed for each. In this way I trust that the essential will be said, and that it will be clearer when disengaged.

Since ecumenism consists in entering into relation with confessions other than one's own so as to promote Christian unity with a common effort, one meets with a preliminary and fundamental question: Should not Catholics agree to deal with non-Catholics on an equal footing? It is understood that here we do not speak of the attitude of the persons. A Christian can never have too much humility and consideration for others. It has to do with doctrine. The Catholic believes, not in the sense of opinion, but with all the certitude afforded him by the faith, that his Church is the sole Church of Christ. Will this conviction which the Catholic ecumenist may not set aside for an instant permit carrying on dialogue, praying in common, or establishing a common end with those who belong to other Christian communities?

Not all Catholic ecumenists answer this question in the same way. Some believe that it is possible and even indispensable to carry out all ecumenical work in full equality. It is true that the Catholic believes that his Church is the sole true Church of Christ. But it is not only he who believes that he alone possesses the truth. For example, Father Couturier writes: "When realized in the soul of a believer, the Catholic faith becomes with respect to the content of his belief, a psychological reality which is similar to the psychological state created in the respective souls of his Protestant, Anglican, or Orthodox brethren by the psychological reality of their respective faiths. One therefore finds that *psychologically*, Catholics, Protestants, or Orthodox find themselves situated, with regard to the problem of Christian unity, in a similar position" ("Prière et Unité chrétienne," quoted in *L'Abbé Couturier*, by M. Villain, p. 357; italics in original).

Father Villain quite rightly uses the term "master idea" for this belief in the identical psychological situation of Christian consciences before the problem of unity (*ibid.*, p. 52). For this reason, we should listen before proceeding further to those who do not admit that this view is either right or useful.

Without any doubt they concede that carefulness in maintaining equality, at least as well as possible, will facilitate contacts with our non-Catholic brethren; that this pleases them very much—indeed much more than the traditional appeal for a return to the Mother Church from which their ancestors once withdrew. It consequently behooves us to compensate for what is less accommodating in doctrine through an understanding of others, and through a redoubling of charity and humility. Moreover, we are dealing with ecumenism: our interlocutors are prepared to see us act and speak according to our own faith. Since it is said that they also think they possess the truth, they will permit us a stand which is similar to their own. Herein lies the big ecumenical difficulty. If it is inherent in the state of separation, it is the part of wisdom to recognize it and thus make the effort to overcome it rather than deny it and let it subsist.

Whatever considerations of the practical order may be, the question remains whether or not all Christians, when they maintain their different confessions, are in the same psychological state. This must be emphatically denied. Being in good faith, they doubtless believe that they possess the truth. Much more so if they have the virtue of faith (as we are allowed to suppose) for all that they see in the light of that faith is certainly true. But do all see everything that they affirm in this light? No. By the light of faith one sees nothing false, and when two Christians are in opposition because of contradictory assertions, one of the two states is an error. He is not conscious of it, but on this point he is not conscious of seeing truth. Whereas the one who sees rightly on this point is conscious of seeing rightly. Fundamentally, we revert to the objection of the skeptics who allege the same psychological state for the one who thinks rightly and the one who is in error. One answers them the same way we do here. The one who is in error does not know that he is in error, but on the point upon which he is mistaken he is not conscious of knowing the truth. If it were otherwise, no one would ever be sure of possessing the truth, and the ecumenical movement could not be justified—it could never come to its proper end. It could not be justified because if each one had full assurance of possessing the truth, uneasiness and dissatisfaction (the causes of search) would not arise—and if the movement were to begin, it would never come to an end. In fact, anyone not satisfied with his certitude of the truth of his confession on a given point would be doubtful of any similar certitude received in a contrary sense on the same point.

Let us speak more concretely. A Protestant affirms that the Catholic Church is in error—that in particular there is nothing which obliges one to believe in the Assumption of the

Blessed Virgin. First of all, if he saw this in the light of faith he would have true certitude, and this nothing can legitimately shake. If he were to change his opinion and if, in dialogue with Catholics, he came to admit the truth of the Assumption of the Mother of God—and if this new certitude were in no way different from the former—what reason would he have for placing confidence in it? If such a change is to be a legitimate one the first certitude must not have been one of faith, but the second must be so.

In the case of the Catholic, all that he is bound to believe on the authority of the Church is seen by him in the light of faith. For the Christian who is not Catholic, there is always some point in what he professes that he does not see in the light of faith—even if it should only be the error which he attributes to the Catholic Church. The certitude which he professes to have on this point is entirely different from that which he has on the great mysteries of the Trinity, the Incarnation, and the Redemption (which a true faith manifests to him). St. Thomas declares that error cannot be believed by faith in these words: "Ratio formalis obiecti fidei est veritas prima; unde nihil potest cadere sub fide, nisi in quantum stat sub veritate prima, sub qua nullum falsum stare potest, sicut non ens sub ente, nec malum sub bonitate" (2-2ae, qu. Ia, art. 3c.)

We will find the same divergences among Catholic ecumenists if we pass to the consideration of the end of the ecumenical movement. Doubtless, everyone accepts it as a return to unity of faith, and this bears with it unity of government and of worship. Those who try to carry out ecumenical work on an equal footing with the other confessions may not present this return as a return to the Catholic Church; this would give the Catholics too great superiority. Let us even suppress this word "return." (It is not necessary, although it is frequently found in the Roman documents—even in the encyclical *Ad Petri cathedram* and in a discourse which the Pope delivered on April 24. Its ordinarily accepted meaning contains nothing offensive.) Should we say "accord" or "union" with the Catholic Church, even this seems to signify some superiority. Wherefore, the difficulty is to be resolved by a double operation.

On the one hand, the non-Catholics will be asked not to leave their confession, but to remain in it, to live it more deeply, to reform themselves, to revivify themselves. Who could refuse such a program for unity's sake? On the other hand, the Catholics will be asked to do the same. Father Couturier formulated his concept thus: "Under the influence of prayer, each member of a Christian group (including the Catholics) will deepen his life, will make use of his talents, will reform himself in whatever way he should be reformed—and will ascend towards the Lord until he reaches that height where the walls of separation come to an end. All will then reciprocally recognize in their other brethren the Christ whom they adore. They will recognize him as he is, identical with himself: one, sole in his love, his life, and in his thought. Then will come the realization of dogmatic unity, the full agreement of all spirits with the sole thought of Christ. And union will proclaim itself through the voice of Peter. Perhaps this will be done in an immense Ecumenical Council" (quoted by M. Villain in *L'Abbé Couturier*, pp. 361-362). This biographer tells us that he "preached nothing else than the attachment of each one to his own Church, and the program of 'spiritual emulation' to make progress toward the unity willed by Christ" (*Ibid.*, p. 185). Since everyone should change, it is not a matter of promoting a union of the Protestant or Orthodox brethren with the Catholic Church as she is today. It will be transformed; all will be transformed. "A revivified Catholicism alone will afford conditions in which the non-Catholic Christians could integrate... Thus we respect the mystery of a progression which will lead us from the impoverished Catholicism of our epoch—already undergoing a magnificent reawakening—toward the fulness of a renewed Catholicism in which all our brethren will find the fulness of their desires" (*Ibid.*, p. 286).

It is upon this vision of unity, which will mean for no one either conversion, renunciation, or denial—but simply, and for all, the achievement of an internal progress, miraculously brought to its term—it is upon this vision, I say, that the formulas propagated by Father Couturier for the January ecumenical week were inspired. All Christians should say the same prayer for unity. The Catholics, then, would not ask for the entrance of their non-Catholic brethren into the Catholic Church, because the others would be unable to say such a prayer. Since the time when convergence of all communions will bring unity is unknown, and the form which will be conferred upon the Church by this convergence and miracle of union is also not known, one prays that God realize unity when He will and by whatever means He wills.

The whole of this concept (quite coherent for anyone who admits its principle) pleases the non-Catholics, and also many Catholics who find it both liberal and generous. Its authors overflow with charity, zeal, piety, and enthusiasm. I should like, for my part, to retain as much as possible of it. But it cannot be denied that it also has its disadvantages, or lacunae, and I must now say a word about these.

First of all, it is true that the more the Catholic Church becomes perfect in its members, the more strongly will it attract the other Christians. This is why the Pope, now gloriously reigning, intends to prepare the way for the progress of unity by celebrating a council which will cast greater splendor upon the titles of the Catholic Church. There are many things which are capable of modification. But these lie in the order of the accidental. The council is not going to construct another Church. Particularly, the dogmas will all remain as subject of firm belief, and their meaning will remain unchanged. If today they are an insurmountable barrier, they will remain so tomorrow also. One may therefore invite Protestants and Orthodox to come to the Roman Church right now, and strive to show them this permanent miracle (ever admired by tradition) of the duration and the activity of the Church.

It is also true that according to the measure of their sanctification the non-Catholics become increasingly attached to the truths which they possess. But will they in like manner also renounce the errors which separate them from the Catholic Church if one does not assist them with other means? This would not follow necessarily. There are examples of non-Catholics whose souls were most beautiful, in so far as one may judge, and who have died without becoming reconciled with the Catholic Church.

On the other hand, since it is supposed that the sanctification which is asked for them will lead them to the Catholic Church, the more loyal and honest thing would be to say it plainly. Otherwise, one would encourage them to dream of a Church of the future which will be different from the Catholic Church of today—and this would hardly dispose them to overcome a separation which is maintained because of essential and permanent elements of our Church.

We are told that when all Christians will ask unity with one identical prayer, and offered by all at the same time, unity will be accomplished by God. Suppose that such unanimity were possible without still another great miracle, how do we know that it will have this efficacity? For this answer a revelation would be required. But above all, as long as the separations last and we understand unity differently, we cannot say the same prayer in asking for unity. Members of the direction of the Faith and Order Commission and other Protestants have understood this. They have understood that it is only possible for us to pray at the same time. Cullmann tells us, "The Catholics themselves ought not to hide from the Protestants that they may not discuss unity with us with that absence of a priori which we may experience when we enter into ecumenical dialogue" (*Catholic et Protestant,* p. 25).

Even so, I willingly recognize that the Catholic ecumenists of whom we speak let it be seen at times that they do have in mind the Catholic Church as the terminus of the ecumenical movement. Thus in the mind of the Abbé Couturier the convergence brought about by the different confessions is indeed a convergence towards the Catholic Church, since the final union will be proclaimed by Peter, according to the text cited above. The fact of the matter is that after all—in spite of the concessions made to egalitarian requirements—they are still guided by faith in the Catholic Church's prerogative.

Until now we have treated of a total concept of Catholic ecumenism. The criticism accompanying our presentation has permitted a sufficient understanding of the position of another trend. This seems to us to be more traditional and to conform better to the pontifical documents. However, we do not wish to define it only by opposition to the preceding method, because there are many points in which the two trends coincide.

First of all, the separated brethren ought to know the immutable truths of the Catholic Church (I refer to the Instruction of the Holy Office, *Ecclesia catholica*) concerning the true nature of justification. Still in the same line, there must be discussion "on the constitution of the Church, on the Roman Pontiff's primacy of jurisdiction, and on the only real union effectuated by the return of the dissidents to the one true Church of Christ." How are they to know this if we do not say it?[1]

With this firmly established, one may very well pray and have others pray for union. One ought not only show toward all the most sincere charity. One should keep close to the historical truth about persons and deeds of the past as of the present. We should judge with kindness the writings of the dissidents and enter into dialogues and conferences with full objectivity. Still more we should seek in adverse doctrines the part which is true, throw it into relief and use it to show how it would be safeguarded and strengthened as part of Catholic doctrine. Also, this should be done without polemics, but with dignified and open apologetics. In this way we will further that convergence of the confessions towards the Catholic Church which is desired by the ecumenists of whom we have spoken.

We may now consider a few particular questions on which there is a certain difference of opinion among Catholic ecumenists.

The great majority of non-Catholic Christians have preserved Baptism. They have the cult of the Holy Bible; they preach the Gospel; they pray and sing beautiful prayers and moving hymns. These are gifts of God by which they receive graces, may live well, and attain their salvation. The Orthodox (who must always be considered apart since they are the brethren closest to us) have preserved the priesthood, and

---

[1]In conversation once with one of the most outstanding theologians of the World Council, the latter told me he thought that the Catholic Church would one day drop one or another of the defined dogmas. The ecumenist might also keep in mind that if the dissidents should know the abovementioned truths, there is all the more reason that the Catholics to whom one speaks of ecumenism should know them.

devotion to Mary and the Saints. What relationship with the Roman Catholic Church results from these gifts which are also known as *vestigia Ecclesiae*? Does it perhaps follow that the members of the dissident churches are also members of the Catholic Church, or that these dissident Churches are also truly and properly Churches?

No one maintains that the dissidents can be members of the Catholic Church in the same sense as the Catholics, because in that case all would be in the same Church and union would be an accomplished fact. It has to do with admitting this in some way. One thing certain is that validly conferred Baptism introduces one into the true Church of its nature. There are some who quote this sentence from the Encyclical *Mediator Dei*: "By the waters of Baptism, as by common right, Christians are made members of the Mystical Body of Christ the Priest" (*AAS* (1947), 555). They arrive at the conclusion that the separated brethren in good faith are members of the Mystical Body, although not in the full sense as are the Catholics. There are others, however, who are of the opinion that this encyclical refers to the natural effect of Baptism—an effect which can be suspended by some cause. They call upon an earlier encyclical, the *Mystici Corporis*, where it is said that: "Only those are really to be included as members of the Church who have been baptized and profess the true faith, and who have not unhappily withdrawn from Body-unity or for grave faults been excluded by legitimate authority." But our separated brethren do not profess the true faith. Moreover, a little further on the same encyclical speaks of these brethren (as they are today) as not belonging to the visible organism of the Body of Christ, and it describes their state in conformity with this fact. They have simply a relation of order to the Mystical Body of the Redeemer through a certain desire and a certain unconscious aspiration. And they are invited to enter the organism of the Body of Christ.

The teaching of this encyclical would therefore appear to be clear. Since it is directly applicable to the matter at hand, it should serve to interpret the other texts. Finally, in the encyclical *Humani Generis*, of still later date than the two others which we have just cited, Pius XII voices this complaint:

"Some say they are bound by the doctrine, explained in Our Encyclical Letter of a few years ago, and based on the sources of revelation, which teaches that the Mystical Body of Christ and the Roman Catholic Church are one and the same" (*AAS* 1950). Nevertheless, it seems to us that the difference between the two opinions is not as great as it might appear at first sight. The bond of desire and of aspiration that the *Mystici Corporis* shows between the dissident Christians and the Mystical Body of Christ (and which permits of eternal salvation while maintaining the validity of the axiom *extra Ecclesiam nulla salus*) signifies perhaps everything that some others place in the term "members not in the full sense."

Still more grave is the question of deciding whether the dissident communities—possessing elements of the true Church—are in so much and as such (that is to say, as communities) objects of divine favor, and are Churches in the proper sense. If such were the case one would have a notion of the Church quite close to that which is now widespread in the World Council of Churches: the Church of Christ is not comprised within one sole Church, but is found in several of differing faiths. The famous branch theory was more moderate. There still remains a difficulty. How can it be that there where there is true Baptism, perhaps other Sacraments, perhaps the Eucharist—where there is the service of Christ, there is no Church?

Indeed, the term Churches is given to the dissident Oriental communities. This is done in order to recognize in them their authentic apostolic succession, and consequently their real though incomplete hierarchy. Still it may not be given in the full sense, since as such they are dissident: and if they constituted a Church, there would be Churches outside the true Church of Christ.

I believe that the true answer is this: where there is Baptism, there is the Church—but it is the Roman Catholic Church. A text of St. Albert the Great (found in the book *Divided Christendom* by Father Congar) reads thus: "The Sacraments are the nest of the Church; and this nest does not belong to the heretics: also when they lay down their little ones, they do not lay them down outside the Church, but within her" (III Sent., d. 6 C, a II, ad I; Congar, p. 288). This is a doctrine which

St. Augustine often inculcated: *Domini nostri habent bona, Ecclesiae habent bona* (*Sermo ad Caesareensis Ecclesiae plebem,* n. 2 Migne 43, 691). "However, the goods which we acknowledge in them are not theirs; they have goods of Our Lord, they have goods of the Church." The person who receives a valid Sacrament outside the Church enters into possession of a good of the Catholic Church; he has not the right to it, but his good faith saves him. Of course, it is within his own confession that he receives this benefit, but it is not by the merit of his confession.

The grace of God falls, therefore, directly upon the individual persons when it is given outside the Catholic Church, and not first upon his "church." Nevertheless, one could think that in certain circumstances (and for a greater good) God favors the interests for example of Protestantism—not in so much as it is opposed to the Catholic Church, but in so much as it has conserved the elements of the Church mentioned above. What God wishes, then, is that his gifts succeed in reaching the men who have been redeemed by Jesus Christ. What he permits is that they reach them by an illegitimate way. What traditional doctrine forbids is extending the Church of Christ, which is his Mystical Body, beyond the Roman Catholic Church. One must also keep in mind that if some Christian elements (such as the frequent reading of the text of the Bible) have been more intensely cultivated within some dissident communities than in the Catholic Church, this particular care—which exceeds that of many Catholics—does not exceed the desire of the Church. It could continue within it without effecting any change of a substantial sort.

Catholic ecumenists hold different opinions on another point. The first act proposed by the Assembly of the World Council of Churches at New Delhi was the proclamation of the integration of the International Missionary Council with the Geneva Council. The Orthodox members of the World Council resisted until 1959. Since then they have let themselves be persuaded, and have given their approbation. Many Catholics declare that they are glad of this integration. One easily understands that the directors of the World Council of Churches would have desired this act, and would have guided their member Churches accordingly. The mission is inherent in the nature of the Church; the Council has helped the Churches to fulfill this essential function. The Council has become an institution which still maintains a certain movement toward unity, but which conducts itself rather like a federation of Churches. I heard the reasons designed to make this integration agreeable to the Orthodox and the Catholics from the mouth of Norman M. Goodall, ex-president of the International Missionary Council and President of the Joint Committee for Integration, as well as from Brother Max Thurian who functions at Geneva. The former was firmly convinced, the latter somewhat less. Firstly, integration will not mean very much of a change, since already almost all the Churches belonging to the International Missionary Council belong also to the World Council, which consequently aided them in their missions. Then, integration is desired for reasons of faith and of organization, and not at all to make obstacles for the Catholic Church. Finally, integration will introduce the ecumenical spirit everywhere. It will combat bad proselytizing, and it will hinder the sects which are at the present time the most dynamic in attempting to invade the Catholic countries. All this, along with other considerations patiently collected by Fr. Leeming in his excellent volume *The Churches and the Church* (pp. 185-207), tends to allay our fears and permit one to await a view of the consequences before forming a conclusive judgment. Nevertheless, I am unable to understand how the aid furnished by the World Council to the Protestant Missions could fail to abet the progress of Protestantism, the enlargement of divisions, and the forming of a still greater obstacle to the Catholic missions. I believe that it would have been wiser, from the ecumenical point of view, to have sought unity first—and with unity to have gained the world for Christ: "Even as thou, Father, in me and I in thee; that they also may be one in us, that the world may believe that thou hast sent me" (Jo. 17:21).

I think I have touched upon the principal questions confronting the Catholic ecumenist—upon which they have at times taken different positions. Since these differences exist it is better to consider them. It is perhaps the best way of attenuating them. It is also a way of making progress. An opinion which springs from sorrow for divisions and love of unity will always contain some valuable element of truth which the man who thinks otherwise is glad to assimilate. Truth is a fundamental good; it does not divide, it unites. It is the bread of the intelligence but one must often earn his bread by the sweat of his brow.

The Layman's Potential for Ecumenism

by Robert W. Hovda

It is interesting and somewhat startling to note the extent to which ecumenism has been accepted (just in the last two years in the American Church) as a properly Catholic concern. Interesting for all of us who feel that the Holy Spirit has not abandoned the modern world. Startling to those of us who had become accustomed to a policy, or at least a practice, of obscurantism and delay on most religious issues touching contemporary man.

This is not the place to discuss the reasons for the wholesale disregard of those habits, customs and attachments which we Catholics so often mistake for genuine tradition. But it is true. Diocesan newspapers (which are still noticeably suspicious of a liturgical revival already so venerable as to be official) are printing with a kind of abandon, week after week, articles about the ecumenical movement and ecumenical activities.

One hopes this is not because our highly denominational news service or our editors are under the mistaken impression that Protestantism is about to surrender. Or under the equally mistaken impression that all of these activities have a direct relation to the Second Vatican Council. Perhaps we can rejoice in the fact, without imputing the motives suggested by our fears and our experience.

Partly as a result of this publicity, partly as a result of deeper spiritual forces at work in the Christian world, a rapidly increasing number of American Catholic laymen are taking an interest in efforts toward reunion. They are beginning to articulate a problem. They are saying: "We know what the theologians must do. We have some idea of what the bishops, the national hierarchies, the clergy should be doing. But is there anything that *we* can do?"

This hesitation and uncertainty, this question, is hardly surprising. Along with the liturgical revival and ecumenism, one of the most important trends in contemporary Catholicism is a gradual re-defining of the specific role of the layman in the Church and in the temporal order. Catholic thinkers generally recognize now that in our feverish efforts to defend the hierarchical ministry these several hundred years we have ignored the layman. And this has resulted in a warped ecclesiology, an idea of the nature of the Church so partial and so incomplete as to be positively misleading. Awaiting a correction of this deplorable state of affairs, this canonizing of apathy, the layman has a right to wonder whether there is anything he can *do*, with regard to this or any other church problem.

Many of the writers in the field of ecumenical affairs think that there is much the layman can do, must do. Indeed, they would go so far as to say that unless the whole body of the Church—at least, its leading spirits and thinkers, many of whom are laymen—becomes alive with this concern the work of bishops and theologians either will not be done or, if done, will be fruitless.

In these paragraphs, then, I would like to summarize a number of the suggestions made by Catholic ecumenists which I think are relevant to the layman's role in promoting efforts toward the great goal of Christian peace and unity. Any classification of these ideas is arbitrary, because they overlap. Which means, of course, that I shall attempt such a classification: 1) lay activity within the Church itself; 2) lay activity in terms of relations between the churches; 3) lay activity in the temporal order.

1. How does the layman promote ecumenism in his role within the Church?

Here we can examine only a few of the more obvious and necessary activities. For it is clear that *anything* which communicates to men, which helps men see, the Church as it is—the Mystical Body of Christ, Christ in his members, living, loving, ministering, forgiving, healing, teaching, uniting—is also, and incidentally, a service to ecumenism. Anything which contributes to that unceasing renewal and reformation so imperative for the Church in its concrete life is also, and incidentally, a service to ecumenism.

To anyone who might be looking for a one-volume encyclopedia of ecclesiastical renewal and reformation, I can suggest nothing better than the acute and penetrating book by Fr. Hans Küng.[1] His whole thesis is that a true reform of the Church is a *sine qua non* of work toward reunion.

A Fraders cartoon pictures two birds huddled in a blizzard on a snow-covered branch of a tree. One of them was saying firmly to the other: "Well, we're not migratory, and that's that." This is not a Catholic posture, but it is the posture of many committed American Catholics, lay and clerical. Until we cleanse ourselves, individually and corporately, of our excessive and emotional attachment to that "old time religion" (which wasn't good enough for grandpa and isn't good enough for us or for our world), there is little hope that we can be of significant use to him whose creation is always new.

a. *Prayer*

I mention prayer as the first activity, because the Church is a community of prayer, because her worship is in every sense *common prayer,* and because her worship is the center of her life. And because a unity which is God-willed, a unity so far beyond human pride, human passions, human prejudices—such a unity must be a grace, a gift, one of those good gifts which come only from "above"—and because one of the reasons our Father permits us to pray, commands us to pray, is that we learn by praying. It is in prayer disciplined by dogma that we learn what we should desire, what we should be working for. It is in prayer which conforms itself to the expressed will of Christ that our wills receive a Christian formation.

[1]This has recently been published as *The Council, Reform and Reunion* (New York, Sheed and Ward), 1961.

Our private prayer will include ecumenism not only as an intention, not only as a frequent petition for that harmony and peace, that love and unity to which the New Testament bears so strong a witness. Perhaps more fundamentally it will be a private prayer which begins with the Word of God, which flows from meditating his Word in the Bible. It will not be chained to set forms, even those of tolerable dignity and soundness, but will have its spontaneous expressions as well.

With regard to public prayer, it would be surprising if the Catholic ecumenist were not already involved in the liturgical revival, in education and petitions and protests to the end that our public worship may become again a religious experience for our people. It would be surprising if he did not see how desperately we need the use of our language in the Eucharist, the Mass, as well as in the auxiliary and lesser sacraments. He will be offering his services and his talents in training the parish for congregational prayer and congregational song, in finding and training lectors and cantors for their ministry of assistance at the altar.

Only when we have this foundation of a revitalized public worship in general will the other means of promoting ecumenism in our congregational services begin to be effective. Then the layman can suggest and encourage the lector's frequent recommendation to the congregation of intentions for Christian unity, intentions concerned directly or indirectly with the quest for peace among Christ's members. He can contribute his ideas for the celebration of specific weeks and seasons of concentration on this problem: the preparation for and celebration of Pentecost; the January week of prayer for unity. And he can participate in them and urge others to participate in them, as well as in the votive mass for unity and in prayers of reparation for sins against unity (e.g., St. Bartholomew's Day, though the possibilities here are legion).

The use of spontaneous prayer in public is an old Catholic custom now, unfortunately, almost totally lost. It must be revived. And it can be revived successfully and with great spiritual gain only by men and women who have thoroughly absorbed liturgical prayer—to the Father, through Jesus Christ, in the Holy Spirit; its simplicity; its emotional control; its doctrinal content. Countless public occasions provide opportunities for this instead of the inevitable formula. And the practice should help restore vitality to the formulae themselves.

One more point in connection with the public worship of the Church. Those public services called "devotions" are still, in most American parishes, utterly at odds with the whole liturgical tradition of the Church. They are retained, say the pastors, because laymen demand them. Can the laity, conscious now of their need for scriptural formation and for authentic (non-exaggerated) common prayer, not ask for public "devotions" of Bible reading, preaching, psalm or hymn responses, congregational prayer (silent or litany form) and then the prayer of the president of the community, the celebrant?[2]

b. *Adult education*

Another great service to ecumenism, the achievement of Catholic maturity, has many facets and all of them are relevant to our problem. We know that the current Protestant "return" to the positive principles of the sixteenth century Reformers has made a more fruitful dialog with Catholics possible. It is also true that the more we grow up in our understanding of our own tradition and move away from the fright and defensiveness which has characterized post-Reformation Catholicism, the better are we prepared for fruitful dialog.

This doesn't mean that we have to reject the spiritual climate and the spiritual culture which is ours today, or that we have to return to some imagined pristine and pre-Reformation form of the Church. What it does mean is that we must study the Gospel, the development of doctrine, church history, sufficiently so that we have at least some grasp of the distinction between the God-given Good News and its Spirit-guided elaboration on the one hand and on the other the limitations of the culture, the language, the historical situation and circumstances through and in which the Good News always comes to concrete men and nations.

---

[2]See Fr. Joseph Connolly's articles in 1962 issues of *Worship* magazine on "Bible Devotions."

If this is difficult, it is also terribly important. Fidelity to Christ demands it. The ecumenical movement can profit from it, indeed cannot exist without it. Cultural forms, folk-lore, legal and disciplinary practices are both enriching and important in the life of every human being. But they vary from community to community, from society to society. A Church which is truly catholic will welcome this diversity and variety of forms in which the Word of God becomes real and intelligible to diverse and various peoples. The uniformity a truly catholic Church demands is minimal.

So the mature Catholic will not presume to chain the Word of God to any one language, no matter how venerable, to any one culture or civilization, to any one set of philosophical categories. He knows too well how a kind of europeanism or americanism or latinism or greekism have dimmed the appeal of the Christ (who belongs to all) to the great peoples of Africa and the Orient. Human greed and proprietorship are bad enough when they infect man's economic and political life. They are disastrous when they corrupt catholic revelation and the means of man's salvation.

The maturity to which laymen (and clergy) are called, then, is a maturity which rejoices in the truth and in the innumerable forms, categories, languages through which men of different times and places both apprehend and share the truth. No provincialism or parochialism will blind us to the frightening fact that it is our human pride and obstinacy as much as anything else that has confined the love and freedom of the Gospel to so small a proportion of the earth's people. The enriching contribution of all those others has yet to be made to a Catholic Church which after 2000 years is overwhelmingly western in locale and pink in complexion.

Religious education, whether of child or adult, is aimed at love as well as knowledge. It should produce a recognition of Christ's call as a call to holiness (i.e., to love) rather than as a call to the "performance" of what are termed "religious duties." Who would dare say that this sanctity, which is love, is irrelevant to hopes for reunion and work for reunion? Here is that attraction of Christ which moves the intellect to the leap of faith. Only afterward does the congruity between human experience and the message of salvation become rationally compelling. Holiness, love, is the fruit which invites men to the tree.

Ecumenism perhaps suffers as much from clumsy efforts at an immature and insufficiently-grounded "apostolate" as from any other defect in the Church. Not every apparently good action is one which should be undertaken immediately. Maturity will see the necessity of abstaining even from good actions if in the long run they may be obstacles to the achievement of a greater good. Scoring a momentary apologetic victory is not always a service to Christ's cause. And if we think of it in terms of "scoring" and of "victory," it is never a service.

There is a valid apostolate which seeks individual conver-ion to and incorporation in the Mystical Body, the Church, and its full sacramental life. But such an apostolate is not the mission of the ecumenical movement. Its work is directed toward corporate reunions and institutional reforms. An immature Catholic may regard this slow and patient work as an evasion of Christian responsibility. Intelligent laymen can make a great contribution to the ecumenical movement if they will only learn to appreciate the difference between the Catholic missionary task and true ecumenism.

I want to make at least one more point in connection with this crying need for a more mature Catholicism. That is the point Karl Rahner, S.J., develops so well in his essay, "Free Speech in the Church," and which receives intelligent attention in the important book *Problems of Authority*. Baptized and confirmed Catholics must learn to feel a responsibility to manifest in the Church generally, and to the hierarchy and clergy in particular, their ideas, opinions, suggestions, their frank criticisms, even their protests—insofar as all these things have a bearing on the life of the Church.

Quite apart from the ecumenical cause, this interplay, this exchange of ideas and of criticism between members of the Church, especially between laity and hierarchy, is necessary for her health and progress. With regard to its bearing on reunion, anyone who has read or listened to an Orthodox or Protestant view of Roman Catholicism knows how pained they are and how suspicious they become because of the passivity and the curious notion of obedience characteristic of so many Catholics.

This implies an understanding rather than a rejection of hierarchial authority. The exercise of authority in the Church is not a simple business of generals and privates. It is much more complex, much more subtle than the army bit. And to ignore this is to invite a repudiation of the structure our Lord has given to his Church (which has happened more than once in history).

c. *Other aspects of the layman's role*

It is more than evident that not all currents of contemporary Catholic life and theology appeal equally to Christians who are not Roman Catholics. Our developing theology on the role of the layman in the Church excites them, but refinements in Mariology leave them cold. While avoiding any distortion of doctrines and any compromise which would offend the integrity of faith, ecumenically-minded Catholics would do well to note these responses. For we believe the Holy Spirit is with them, too. To say nothing of the fact that the theology of the laity is evoking a tremendous response within the community of the Catholic faithful as well.

I have already commented on two aspects of this rediscovery of the layman: his role in the public worship, the liturgy of the Church (liturgical revival); and his role in criticism and public opinion within the Church. But these roles do not exhaust the layman's responsibility. The common belief of the faithful is, in Newman's view, one of the proofs of right doctrine, one of the evidences of the Holy Spirit's direction. Though in the realm of doctrinal development the hierarchy judges, it judges in communion with and paying close attention to that faith which compels the minds and moves the hearts of all Christ's members.

And then there is the matter of lay consultation in determining the policies and programs of parish and diocese and world church. The action of some Dutch bishops in establishing advisory councils of elected laymen from their parishes; Archbishop Shehan's invitation to the laity to send suggestions by letter for the Baltimore synod; Cardinal Koenig's appeal to laymen to speak their minds with regard to the forthcoming ecumenical council—these are all contemporary indications of a return to an earlier Catholic practice of teamwork and cooperation and pooling of both clergy's and laity's ideas in matters of Church government.

Enough work has been done by theologians (Congar, Rahner, etc.) in these areas to establish a good number of ideas for laymen to tangle with, to ponder, to discuss . . . and to bring to the attention of those who do not share their faith in its fullness. For the latter have long been convinced that Catholic laymen are, by some exigency of their faith, merely passive onlookers in a clerical Church. One wonders if the problem of authority would loom so large in their minds if they were to understand fully by what process of reaction we arrived at our practice of the last several centuries and what hopes there are for a more authentic practice in the future.

Perhaps Protestant rejection of authority in the Church is not that at all, but a rejection of the ecclesiastical proletariat to which their notion of Catholic authority (and our practice of it in recent centuries) has reduced the Christian laity.

d. *The scope of morality*

Ecumenism is too authentically Christian a movement to encourage any romantic ideas about ridding the world of sin. Wheat and tares grow together, and they grow together in each of us and in all of us. But the ecumenical movement is concerned about relating the Christian message to the great moral problems of our time. And Catholic laymen who would promote it must be prepared to re-educate themselves morally and to broaden immensely the scope of that "morality" which so many of us learned by rote.

At a parish meeting recently a layman expressed his view that the greatest moral problem confronting the Church in America is the problem of "racial" prejudice, discrimination, segregation. The pastor became incensed and shouted, "You're wrong—the greatest moral problem confronting the Church in America is *immorality!*" One dares not laugh. Nor does one dare ask, "What is immorality?" You know the answer.

Whatever the reason and however we got this way, our "morality" is almost exclusively a private affair and effectively restricted to the sphere of sex (an important sphere, but only one). The great social questions of war and disarmament, of racial and national intergroup tensions and injustices, of poverty in the midst of abundance, of the social responsibility that goes with power—these are hardly thought of as moral questions. We have "duties" toward God, but somehow they don't seem to involve our fellow-man. We have no moral duties toward our neighbor except to refrain from showing him more or less lewd pictures.

I hope this is a highly exaggerated picture. I am not sure that it is. The layman must be allowed to surmount this fixation on sex, must lift his eyes compassionately to see *all* of the problems of a tormented and sin-laden humanity, so that with Christ and in Christ he can speak to it *relevant* words of healing and forgiveness. Until then, his child's religion can no more speak the language of ecumenism than it can speak . . . Latin.

And he must see this morality as a loving response to the love of God, a love which persists and is constant even when his response is inadequate or perverse. A legalistic notion of morality simply does not square with the Gospels. And it is totally incongruous with Paul's teaching. Christian morality is not a series of hurdles which man must leap before he arrives at God's mercy. God's mercy is first in the process; it has priority. And we keep trying to respond with love . . . but always whether in success or failure, with the encouraging and exhilarating assurance that his mercy remains.

e. *Can Catholicism be modern?*

What a curious question to ask about the religion of Jesus Christ! He is the Eternal Word, ever new, ever fresh, as much at home in one civilization, one culture, one language as in another. And as much at home in one epoch, one age, one generation as in another. Always contemporary, reigning forever as Son of Man, Prime Man, Head of the human race, his saving work is catholic, universal—vertically in time as well as horizontally in earthly space.

How does it happen then that he so often appears to our age as one whose interests are strictly agrarian, whose idea of etiquette is medieval court ceremonial, who thinks in terms of the essences of things rather than in terms of the concrete, who abhors practically everything about modern life and modern man, from our art and architecture and music to our languages, our cities and our clothing?

It happens because we are his Mystical Body, because he reaches out to this generation, to the men and women and children of the twentieth century through us. We supply his face, his clothing, his language (whether it be speech, literature, art or music), his mode of approach, his cast of mind. And though Christ loves our age and our contemporaries, many of us are more in love with the past, its fossils and its monuments, than we are with the human beings of the present. We can always find excuses for this, but the responsibility remains heavily, inescapably ours.

The problems of the religious orders, the hierarchy and clergy, in this matter are all too obvious. We haven't space to rehearse them here. But the layman, too, bears a small share of guilt. And his atonement can be a service to the Church as well as to ecumenism. After all, he is closer to the modern world, its thought, its ways, than those of us who have come to regard it as a virtue to be remote. He is better able to assess our failures of communication with regard to any of the forms mentioned above.

Laymen, then, must put aside that stilted ecclesiastical language so dear to many of them, and a semi-Latin vocabulary, that they may speak easily of God and faith in the idiom of the day. In their homes they need not mimic the "art" in our churches but can patronize those few artists to whom the world of the sacred has grudgingly granted an uneasy employment. They can recognize that nothing we Christians can say about this age, apart from its capacity for destruction and wholesale murder, is much different from what could have been said about many previous ages. And that indeed the modern world has much to recommend it, from a deeply Catholic and Christian point of view.

I think we could say that Fr. Küng's statement (in the book mentioned above) is modest: "The Church has not been, during her second millenium, the intellectual avant-garde, as she was, on the whole, during her first thousand years."[3]

f. *Wanted in the Church: lay professional competence*

If the suggestions already offered here are valid, it is apparent that the Church has great need of technical and professional lay competence. She has need of masters of English literature who can make her liturgy resound with the nobility of the English tongue at its best. She has need of architects who in wood and steel and concrete and all accessible genuine materials can raise houses of worship which will carry our children forward, not backward. She has need of artists who in sculpture and painting and imagery of every kind can convey the idea of the holy to generations yet to come. She has need of educators who can aid in filling these huge "plants" of ours with the exciting hum of free search and unafraid inquiry. This list could be expanded indefinitely.

It isn't that we lack these people. We have them in the Church and in our parishes. But for the most part we haven't indicated that we want and need their services. There are many reasons for this besides clerical paternalism. I suppose finances would be the one most frequently mentioned. But laymen who love the Church must find ways so to insinuate themselves into her operating machinery that they become indispensable. Perhaps it will begin with volunteer and occasional advice and services.

Fr. Dumont in his book, *Approaches to Christian Unity,* shows how just one of these professions can make an inestimable contribution to the ecumenical movement. He suggests that perhaps many of the needs that religious schisms and splinter-groups meet are as much sociological as theological. So he recommends the employment by dioceses (and perhaps by

---

[3]*Op. cit.,* p. 18.

national hierarchies) of sociologists to study these groups and also to evaluate through research the success of institutions and structures in the Church. In this way the Church can create within herself, without the sacrifice of anything essential, a variety of ways of meeting the sociological needs of people.

g. *Child education: Catechetics*

The catechetical movement, deeply influenced by modern Biblical scholarship and sound educational psychology, is in the process of reforming and renewing our presentation of and education in the truths of faith. New materials are beginning to appear which, instead of presenting a series of truths to be believed and a series of commandments to be obeyed and a series of ritual acts to be "performed," are a call to discipleship, to a personal commitment to a personal God.

Not that dogmas or commandments or the sacramental acts of worship are ignored. But they are related always to Jesus Christ and to the love of God for us, of which Jesus is the great sacrament, the great sign. The teaching of religion then becomes a real proclamation of good news, news of love, forgiveness, eternal life; and dissection and speculation are left to the science of theology where they belong.

Laymen who are teaching religion in Catholic schools or CCD classes and all parents instructing their children can contribute significantly to ecumenism by acquainting themselves with this approach and with these methods, for Protestants too are rediscovering and reaffirming this Biblical method of teaching. Children who have the advantage of training along the lines of, e.g., Herder and Herder's series of "The Catholic Catechism," will be much more prepared than most of us are to enter into a real dialog with other Christians.

h. *Suffering as a service to ecumenism*

If the suggestions so far have been so vague that they only increase the pain of the committed Catholic, perhaps we need to remind ourselves that the religion of the Cross refuses to stop with the merely negative aspects of suffering. Küng says in the work cited: "Anyone who has never, as a member of the Church, suffered on account of the Church, has never known her as she really is or never loved her."[4]

He speaks of three aspects of suffering which can have a tremendously positive value for the work of reunion: suffering with one another in the Church and because of the Church (sensitiveness to our own faults); suffering with those not of our communion (refusing to rejoice in the faults of others); suffering with each other over the act of separation and division.

2. How does the layman promote ecumenism in our relations with other churches?

a. *Effort to know and understand Protestants, Orthodox, Anglicans.*

I do not mean, of course, that all interested Catholics are bound to undertake a full-scale study of their theologies, but rather that, according to each one's opportunities and capacities, there is an obligation not to remain ignorant of this fundamental area in the lives of those with whom we live and work and conduct our society. And the best way to know them is to start talking to them—not about cars and the weather, but about faith and what faith means to them.

This means, too, a particular effort to grasp their language, their way of expressing spiritual and supernatural realities. We can't afford merely to interpret the words they speak in the categories of our own Catholic thought. We have to grasp more than isolated ideas . . . the whole reality of their religious life, if that is possible.

It is certainly good in such conversations to emphasize those "elements" of the Catholic Church which remain in existence in churches separated from her, to search them out and give them full credit, to refuse to minimize or belittle them. But to have genuine understanding we must place those elements of the Church in the whole context of the other's spiritual life.

[4] *Ibid.*, p. 39f.

We must come to see that they "belong" somehow, for the individual involved, in his total view, and that we are not asking something simple or easy when we invite him to keep those elements and discard the rest of his tradition.

What about the dangers of this effort? Our spiritual leaders have in the past strongly discouraged us from inquiring into the nature of the Protestant religious experience. The reason, of course, is a protective one: to safeguard those whose lack of theological education limits their capacity for discernment. But what we sometimes forget is that the danger here is clearly marked and labelled. We are studying something which is called Protestantism or Orthodoxy or Anglicanism or Lutheranism. We are not venturing into some kind of forest of the unknown. And we must avoid the hypocrisy which has unintentionally marked our underscoring of this danger.

Sometimes we talk and think as if Catholic laymen led the sheltered lives of clergy and religious. They are not sheltered. They are plunged every day into a world which is sometimes blatantly atheist, sometimes aware of greater dimensions, sometimes sensual, sometimes restrained, sometimes crudely commercial, sometimes respectful of human values. If we really think that we can protect Catholics from dangers to their faith by banning a few books or by discouraging a dialog with Protestants, we are more naive than any human being has a right to be.

Danger is here to stay. The only rational question is: will our response be stubbornly to keep on sticking helpless fingers into the leaky dike that protects our island ghetto . . . or will it be to learn how to swim? This is not a cavalier answer to a serious question. It is a serious answer to a question which is proposed either with insufficient seriousness or with insufficient integrity.

One quite possible means of initiating this process toward understanding among laymen, besides individual contacts and reading, is the kind of small group with which the Una Sancta movement was born in Germany. These were informal gatherings of neighbors whose purpose was to seek some appreciation of the religious experience of each other. It should go without saying that love as well as knowledge is the goal of such exchanges.

b. *Encouragement of theological conversations*

The part of most of us in this will be simply to create an atmosphere in which this strictly theological dialog between experts will be demanded as well as encouraged. I mentioned above that in Germany this movement began on a popular level, only later involving professional theologians. It began with small groups of Lutherans and Catholics praying for unity and talking about it. The work of theologians (at least ideally) is always partially determined by the needs and interests of the times in which they live.

c. *Formal inter-group relations*

The clergy will be most deeply involved in this area, but the layman should not feel excluded. He can pick up the marvellous challenge issued by the Protestant theologian, Oscar Cullmann. Years ago Cullmann suggested that, merely as a means for the creation of an atmosphere favorable to ecumenism, Protestant groups in an area should take up an annual collection for the poor of the neighboring Catholic parish and Catholic groups should do the same for the Protestant poor. Wherever this has been practiced (many parishes in Europe and some in this country), the results of so simple yet significant a gesture have been deeply moving to all concerned. My own reaction is that this is a stroke of genius which every Catholic layman interested in ecumenism should suggest and push strongly in his area.

A number of Catholic parishes now have laymen officially commissioned for various public relations tasks: contacts with the diocesan paper; representation to the secular press of the community; liaison work with community clubs, lodges, groups. Why could not a layman undertake in each parish the task of keeping in contact with other churches (non-Roman Catholic) in the area, informing them of such parish activities as might interest them, and informing his own parish and its organizations of events social or cultural in the Protestant or Orthodox churches of the neighborhood in which Catholics should be interested?

d. *Minimal expectations for unity*

I think I have already rather explicitly implied this in much that has been said above. But it is an important point. Karl Rahner puts it clearly:

> There is danger that, particularly in controversial theology, a neurotic fear that we are perhaps not 'really,' not 'in our furthest depths,' at one, may destroy such unity as might well exist. Such a fear then gives birth to that strange determination . . . to prove the existence of disagreement by dint of ever more subtle and precise formulations. . . . What seems like a purely verbal and artificial unity may often be the one and only thing possible to men in face of the inconceivable Mystery. . . . We should not, then, say at once of every formula of agreement: Oh, yes, but just go a little deeper into it and discrepancies will soon appear; the general terms in which it is stated are simply hiding them! As though we could not have the very same suspicion about all the unity within the Catholic Church![5]

3. How does the layman promote ecumenism through his temporal activity?

a. *Problems of religious tolerance and Church-State relations*

Despite the fact that the weight of contemporary theological opinion in the Catholic Church is overwhelmingly in favor of what we call the separation of Church and State, these problems are very real in Protestant views of Catholicism and consequently in the ecumenical movement. The suspicion that we Catholics do not respect the consciences of men and that we are only biding our time until we can deny them civil rights, however absurd it may seem to us, will live for a long

[5]Quoted in Küng, *ibid.*, p. 120.

time in Protestant hearts. We can do nothing about the historical reasons for this except to point to those past circumstances which explain, though they do not justify, collective intolerance and repression. We can do nothing about present reasons for this in isolated quarters of our world except to apologize, to beg forgiveness from God and from our brothers, and to press for a more official and universal clarification of the principles involved.

The Catholic layman must bring to his neighbor the knowledge that his suspicions are unfounded, that his "tolerance" (better, *love*) of his disagreeing brother is based on the human and Christian fact that persons have inalienable rights and that they must act on the basis of their own consciences, not on the basis of the Catholic's conscience. And he must make it clear that this respect and love have a public and social as well as a private dimension.

In public life, tolerance and mutual respect are requirements of an improved grasp of the meaning of freedom of conscience, a more theological attention to the personal nature of the act of faith, and a clearer recognition of the proper distinction between the sacred and the secular. The civil government as such simply lacks competence in the field of religion, revelation, the supernatural. It should make no judgments of that kind. It is enough that it serve the worldly common good of men.

b. *Cooperation on non-religious levels*

This seems elementary enough, but it may be the necessary condition and may help create the necessary climate for a properly ecumenical dialog to follow. It is elementary because we are, with our brothers of differing beliefs, members of the same communities, citizens of the same cities and countries. Yet in many places, if you check the lists of those actively involved in the important civic organizations—the political parties, civil rights and civil liberties groups, philanthropic causes, associations concerned with peace, with mental health, with alcoholism, with community improvement on many levels

—you will find that the percentage of Catholics in the communities involved is higher than the percentage of Catholics among those committed to these civic tasks.

It may be a partial explanation but it is no answer to say that once we were not welcome. Part of the answer is certainly in the moral myopia we have already discussed. In view of the fact, how can those who differ in faith help but regard the Catholic laity as queer, as withdrawn, as irresponsible, as coveting an isolation that is harmful to the interests of the community as a whole? And how much is lost to these groups by the absence of so many disciples of Jesus Christ?

c. *Taking the secular and the worldly seriously*

A favorite refuge of those whose vision of life is severely restricted to the material, to what one can taste, touch, smell, see, hear, is the accusation that Catholics, because of their other-worldly aim and goal, cannot possibly take this world and this life seriously. Even (and here we come to ecumenism) our Protestant brothers, who also have a broader and a spiritual view of human existence, suspect sometimes that we are not really interested in this "space-between," in the secular and the temporal.

But faith does not absolve the layman of his temporal tasks. He is truly of the world as well as of Christ, for Christ is the Lord of the world. So he must assume the common human task of competency and knowledge in the field in which he works. The fact that one accepts the ultimate and the transcendent does not mean that one rejects all lesser values. On the contrary, these lesser values, these secular and worldly values, are enhanced the moment they are drawn into the pattern of redemption.

So part of the layman's function is to plunge himself into the human community. No one has the right to "sit this one out." No one has the right to sit around being a Christian. A Catholic is a human being whom God has placed in this world and who must be, therefore, either married or single, a shoemaker or doctor or housewife or carpenter or teacher or lawyer or writer, etc. And who, since he is part of the human community, must be interested in what the sociologist and the political scientist and the economist have to say.

These aren't little extra-curricular activities that are reluctantly permitted the Christian as long as they don't interfere with his prayers. They are precisely what it means to be a man or woman with the layman's function. For the mastery that the Christian exercises here over creation is for the man of faith more than a natural function—it is part of the restoration of all things in Christ. The layman does not have to excuse himself for his engagement and involvement with the temporal. God expects this of him.

And his whole-hearted presence here, with the special gifts he brings (he sees by faith the end, the purpose, the consummation of it all), can be a most important contribution to reunion with other Christians who are also committed to the temporal . . . and to the ultimate gathering of all men in the fellowship of a dynamic and enlivening faith.

I think that these suggestions are all relevant to the layman and to his potential contribution to the ecumenical search for understanding and (we hope) eventual reunion. And I think they are important for our holiness, our discipleship to Jesus Christ, for the inner life of the Church, even were they to be ineffective for ecumenism. But I do not claim that they are exhaustive in any sense. Any intelligent reader will have his own insights into the problems and the possibilities, and perhaps will have more specific proposals to add.

The Holy Spirit has stirred up in the Church today (not only in many laymen but also in many clergy and religious) some rather unusual manifestations of vigor and life and hope: a perhaps unprecedented desire for basic reform and renewal. May the same Spirit nourish these manifestations, ease all frustrations and guide us toward unity as God wills it.

The Present Direction of the Non-Catholic Ecumenical Movement

by Bernard Leeming, S.J.

1. *The difficulty of the subject*

The very title of this essay indicates one serious difficulty, that of choice of language. When a number of Anglo-Catholics in 1947 wrote a booklet called *Catholicity: A Study of the Conflict of Christian Traditions in the West,* a number of Freechurchmen replied in 1950 by a booklet entitled *The Catholicity of Protestantism.* This sets the question: Who are to be called "non-Catholics"? Are the Eastern Orthodox Churches to be called "non-Catholic," or the "Old Catholic" church of Holland? Are "Anglo-Catholics" to be called "non-Catholics"? All of these would, I know for certain, resent very strongly the appelation "non-Catholic": and yet it might be argued that in strict theology they must be considered to be non-Catholics, since they do not accept the sole principle of unity in the one and only Catholic Church.

In spite of this, I confess I should not use the term "non-Catholic" of the Orthodox or of the Anglo-Catholics, mainly to avoid needless offence, and, I think, profitless offence; and I think I should say the same of the Old Catholics of Holland, even though there have been very considerable Protestant influences among them. In December 1900 Father Paul Wattson (then an Episcopalian) "informed Bishop Coleman (Protestant Episcopal) of the strong Catholic position which the Society of the Atonement now held," and I think that up to 1909 Father Wattson of Graymoor would have been pained at being called a "non-Catholic." In fact, the magisterium of the Church has given indications that it is wise to avoid words and language which may offend. The *Instruction* of the Holy Office of 1950 (dated 1949, but not published until 1950) does not use the words "heretic" and "schismatic" and "sect." Moreover, the Holy Father, John XXIII, has been cited—and cited authoritatively—as saying, in an admonitory tone, "Sempre la cortesia, sempre la cortesia." I use the term "non-Catholic," then, as meaning "our separated brethren," and as in fact including all those who are within the World Council of Churches, such as the Orthodox as well as the ecclesiastical bodies, like the Southern Baptist Convention, the Regular Baptists and the Missouri Synod Lutherans, the Adventists, the Pentecostalists and the "sects," who remain without the World Council.

This difficulty about the use of the word 'Catholic' is merely one illustration of the difficulty in finding language which is understood in the same sense by all Christians. This is particularly clear in the differences in the meaning of words like *revelation*, *inspiration*, *tradition*, *atonement*, *justification*, *predestination*, *grace*, *sacrament*, *real presence*, *penance*, *ordination*, *authority*, *merit*, *infallibility*, *person* and others; they are understood differently by Catholics and by Protestants and, indeed, by different groups of Protestants. Part of the difficulty arises from different languages, v.g. the word *Order* in English, when translated into French as *Constitution* misses some of the overtones in the English. The English word *fellowship*—a word used to excess in modern ecumenism—is difficult to translate into French, German, Italian or Spanish. The word "churchly unity" was used in one draft of a Faith and Order paper, and was accepted until Archbishop Ramsey pointed out that it could easily be confused with "churchy," especially in translation. Protestants come of many different traditions, and have difficulty in understanding the real meaning of language used by those of different traditions, v.g., the Lutheran, the Calvinist, the Anglican, the Methodist, the Baptist; they have no common language like Latin and no common frame of reference such as we have in the medieval theologians like St. Thomas and St. Bonaventure. It is not without significance that Greek words are beginning to be used, in transliterated form: *eirénic* (peaceful), *martyria* (witness), *kerygma* (proclamation), *paradosis* (tradition), *episcopé* (oversight), *diakonía* (service), *oikonomía* (stewardship or dispensation), *koinonía* (communion or fellowship), *hagiásmos* (sanctification), *hypómone* (endurance), *homología* (one confession), *anamnésis* (remembrance or memorial), *kenósis* (emptying), *charísma* (special grace or gift), *agapé* (Christian love), *exousía* (authority or commission), *leitoúrgos* (priest-worshipper or sacrificer). The use of these Greek words, taken from the New Testament, is sometimes mere affectation or pedantry; but sometimes the Greek words are used to avoid the connotations of English words, as for instance, *love*, which is used often in a debased sense; *service, fellowship*, which are also used without religious overtones; and *memorial* and *remembrance* are admitted to be inadequate translations of the Eucharistic *anamnésis*.

However, I mention this in passing, to illustrate the difficulty of communication: that is, of understanding the real mind of separated brethren and of making them understand ours. I am far from suggesting that we give up our own terminology, but I think that for people who have studied little Aristotle and no scholasticism we can begin by avoiding technical terms, so as to enter in by their door to lead them out by ours.

How representative are Protestant and Orthodox theologians?

Another difficulty is to know when a Protestant, or even an Orthodox, theologian speaks merely for himself, and when he represents his community or a number of others who are influential. Fr. Weigel remarks that Paul Tillich speaks only for himself and the same is true of many others. It is true of many Orthodox, some of whom have been said to sing out of tune. To some extent one can judge how far individuals are representative by consideration of the choice of topics which are of current interest, by reviewers of books in journals of different tendencies, and, as will appear a little later, by "agreed statements" of groups of theologians, and/or by organs of the Faith and Order Commission and of the World Council. Protestants of all complexions are very conscious of the fact that the insights of the leaders do not easily penetrate down to the mass, and they are making it a special aim to popularize their ecumenical outlooks and insights as much as possible.

An instance of the difficulty of knowing Orthodox doctrine was provided by a meeting some years ago at Fordham between Orthodox and Catholic theologians. A Catholic professor read a paper citing many Orthodox statements about various doctrines; when he had ended, an Orthodox theologian rose and said: "Everything that has been said is correct, according to the documents and authorities cited. But these authorities do not represent the real mind of the Orthodox Church and therefore the conclusions are not acceptable."

I suspect that the authorities included the *Orthodox Confession* of Peter Mogila, the writings of Dosithéos, and the Decrees of the Council of Jerusalem of 1672. Professor Georges Florovsky, in a paper in 1960 by the Faith and Order Commission of the World Council of Churches, in a symposium entitled *Orthodoxy,* says: "It is utterly misleading to single out certain propositions, dogmatic or doctrinal, and to abstract them from the total perspective in which they are meaningful and valid. It is a dangerous habit just to handle 'quotations' from the Fathers and even from the Scriptures, outside of the total structure of faith, in which only they are truly alive. 'To follow the Fathers' does not mean simply to quote their sentences. It means *to acquire their mind,* their *phrónema.* The Orthodox Church claims to have preserved this *phrónema* and to have theologized *ad mentum Patrum.*" For this reason many Orthodox do not regard the works of Jugie and of Spacil as truly representing Orthodoxy. This is exasperating for a Catholic theologian, used to definite and clear statements; at the same time, Florovsky has a point, viz., that the inner spirit and full context of the spiritual life does affect the real meaning of separate propositions. One is thus left in the dilemma: either to write about the spirit and ethos of Orthodoxy, and be accused of generalities and perhaps of vagueness, or to document each statement by quotations from Fathers and Councils, and be accused of "piece-meal" theologizing and of failing to take account of the full context. This same dilemma faces a Catholic theologian when dealing with Protestantism; an old professor of mine used to say: "It is a proof of God's omniscience that he can understand the Anglicans,"—and there is much truth in the remark.

2. *Characteristics of recent Protestant outlooks*

a. *Loyalty to "Reformation principles" as distinct from loyalty to the verbatim* dicta *of the Reformers or to Confessions of Faith*

As regards the various doctrines held by the Reformers, Luther, Zwingli, Calvin, Cranmer, Knox, etc., I think that there are few modern Protestant scholars who would agree fully with any one of them, with the sole exception perhaps of the rejection of papal supremacy. It would not be difficult to adduce a *catena* of Protestant scholars who hold doctrines different from the four main Reformers on points such as the following: the sufficiency of Scripture alone as the rule of faith; justification by faith (really, hope) alone; the penal substitution theory of the Atonement; the doctrine of Predestination by God's "awful decree"; the doctrine of total corruption by original sin; the purely psychological efficacy of sacraments; the purely symbolic presence of Christ in the Eucharist; the reduction of the Eucharistic worship to a mere remembrance of the Passion; the ministry conceived as a purely preaching office; the absolute autonomy of the local congregation (as held by the early "Independents" as distinct from the "national" form of Protestantism); the denial of any reverence to be paid to saints; the complete neglect of honor to the Virgin Mary, mother of God; and even the rejection of prayers for the dead. As authority for this statement that the Reformers' doctrine is no longer regarded as normative, I refer to the volumes prepared for the Lund Conference and published by the Student Christian Movement Press (London, 1951, 1952), entitled: *The Nature of the Church, Ways of Worship, Intercommunion, The Church,* and *The Lund Conference on Faith and Order,* edited by Oliver S. Tomkins, now Bishop of Bristol. But much other evidence could be added.

As regards the Protestant "Confessions of Faith," such as the Schmalcaldic Articles, the Augsburg Confession, the Westminster Confession, the Thirty-Nine Articles of the Church of England, I merely recall some of the language used in them which is no longer heard among the higher ranges of Protestantism, though in what has been called "the Protestant underworld" similar things are heard:

Westminster Confession: "the Pope of Rome . . . is that anti-Christ, that man of sin, and son of perdition that exalteth himself in the church against Christ, and all that is called God" 25:6.

Same: "transubstantiation . . . hath been and is the cause of manifold superstitions, yea, of gross idolatries." "The sacrifice of the Mass . . . is most abomnibly injurious to Christ's one only sacrifice, the sole propitiation for all the sins of the elect" 29:2 and 6.

The Thirty-Nine Articles called "sacrifices of Masses blasphemous fables and dangerous deceits" (art. 31). Such statements could be multiplied. They were accompanied, as is well known, by the most bitter persecution, carried out ruthlessly and savagely.

The change of tone among Protestants—to a notable extent accompanied by a change of tone among Catholics, since many recent Catholic historians, like Erwin Iserloh, Josef Lortz and others, write in far different fashion from Denifle and Grisar—is to be noted as well by what they do not say as by what they say. The old abuse of Catholic doctrines has disappeared—at least among the more learned wing of Protestants. This may be due partly to politeness, but there is considerable evidence that it is at least partly due to a rethinking of the issue involved.

Stages of Protestantism

Protestantism—to make a summary far too hasty and far too generalized—went through these stages:

1. The vehement and controversial rejections of Catholic doctrines and of the whole Catholic synthesis from 1516 or so onwards throughout the sixteenth century.

2. The period of Protestant scholasticism. This was the work of third-generation Protestants, represented in the works of people like Heinrich Heppe, whose *Reformed Dogmatics*, published in 1861, translated into English 1950, cites many of the Protestant scholastics, practically none being later than 1670.

In England, however, the seventeenth century is marked by "the Caroline divines"—Andrewes, Laud, Bramhall, Thorndike, Jeremy Taylor and others—who held a "high" doctrine in many matters. These are regarded as forerunners of the Tractarians and of the Anglo-Catholics.

3. The latter part of the seventeenth century, and practically the whole of the eighteenth century was marked by the rise and influence of German Pietism, tending to a certain mysticism, begun by Philipp Jacob Spener (1635-1705), and continued in Germany by the Moravians, among whom Count Zinzendorf was most prominent (died 1760). This was partly a reaction against the aridity of the scholasticism and an emphasis on the need of holiness. John Wesley (1703-1791) was influenced by Zinzendorf; the Methodists arose in enthusiastic efforts at complete holiness and piety.

4. The nineteenth century (speaking very broadly, for the divisions here made are most sketchy and unduly systematic) was marked by the increasing influence of rationalism and of "biblical criticism." The theologians tended to follow the latest philosophic fashion, v.g. Evolutionism, Kantian or other Idealism, Hegelianism, and so on. The "critical" school, Strauss, Bauer and many others, down to Schweitzer about 1910, were what is called "liberal," denying the real infallibility of the Bible and the New Testament, particularly about the miracles and the divinity of Christ. At the same time, the influence of "liberalism," though deleterious in destroying faith in Christ's true deity, did shake a good deal of the "protestant" convictions, v.g. about verbal inspiration, justification by faith alone, predestination in a Calvinistic sense and penal substitution theories of the Atonement. Errors of one kind not seldom tend to correct errors of another kind.

5. "Neo-Orthodoxy," often associated with Karl Barth, though in fact springing from a variety of causes and people, rejected "liberalism," and returned to a good deal of the older "protestantism," though in a refined form; its main influence has been to insist on the fact of a true revelation from God, even though this is put in terms of a "personal encounter with God, the wholly Other" which can be reduced to excessive subjectivism.

The revolt from "liberalism" can be seen in the different attitude shown towards St. John's Gospel. Writers and commentators like Armitage Robinson (1908), F.W. Scott (1906), F.C. Burkitt (1906), B.W. Bacon (1910), Streeter (1924) and many others argued with considerable show of learning that St. John the Apostle was not the author and that the Gospel was written at a late date, perhaps as late as 150 A.D. But more modern scholars tend to accept the Apostle as the author and to assign the date as before the year 70 A.D. or not long after, v.g. Bernard (1928), Hoskyns (1940), C.K. Barrett (1955), E.B. Redlich (1939), C.H. Dodd (1954), W.F. Albright (1956), and others.

Loyalty to "Protestantism"

Nevertheless, in spite of rejection or neglect of the *dicta* of the actual "Reformers" and of the Reformation Confessions of Faith, and in spite of the turning away from Liberalism, I have found a deep-rooted loyalty to "Reformation principles" and to "Protestantism"; and I have found it very difficult to make precise exactly to what this loyalty is given, and exactly what is its ground and its content. I think it is largely an unconscious or semi-conscious feeling that the "Reformers" were in fact great heroes who led a revolt against tyranny and corruption in the Church and that, though they may have been wrong in many details and in their manner of proceeding, they yet stood for liberty of spirit, for trust in the ordinary man, for the direct access of each man to God, and, above all, for the Bible as against merely human traditions. Men who are divided among themselves, as are Episcopalians, Lutherans, Baptists—divided very radically in doctrine and manner of church government, divided as "Fundamentalists" and "Liberals" —will yet all share this feeling, this sentiment, of loyalty to "the Reformation."

Is this feeling—for it cannot be regarded as an informed and clear judgment—merely the negative one of antagonism to, or disapproval of, the Catholic Church? It would seem to be largely so, though I do not think it is consciously always so. New translations of the works of Luther, Calvin and other

"Reformers" are appearing in English, and I think that the impulse behind this is not merely the desire to renew attacks upon the Church, though this may be so in some cases. A man like Gordon Rupp, who specializes in Reformation history and theology, judges, I think, that the Reformers have something positive to say to men of today, though one cannot easily say what exactly it is. Fr. Weigel gave the best brief statement of Protestantism in its positive aspect that I have seen: "it can be said that the Protestant principle consists of three interrelated propositions. It is an affirmation that God must be experienced immediately in an experience which is non-conceptual and whose intellectual content is not central nor specific. Because it is primary, it is self-standing and self-justifying. The second proposition states that the conceptual expression of the vague intellectual content which will necessarily follow on the experience, is a task which the believer must perform in freedom. This freedom is not absolute. Hence the third proposition which declares that there is a check, and that check is the biblical test. The conceptual expression of the epistemological content of the experience must be expressed in biblical terms."[1]

Now I repeat: this statement of Fr. Weigel's seems to be the best positive summary of the "Protestant" principle that I have seen. And yet Fr. Weigel himself would probably agree that Protestantism is such a protean phenomenon that any generalization is open to many exceptions, and that the statement applies perhaps to Methodists, Lutherans and churches and sects of a congregationalist polity, more clearly and generally than it applies to Calvinists and Presbyterians, and to many Anglicans. Moreover, the analysis of the act of faith made by some Catholics, v.g. Aubert, would go far towards accepting the first proposition, viz. that the ultimate ground of faith can scarcely be put into conceptual categories.

An analysis of Protestantism

I should be inclined to modify a little Fr. Weigel's analysis of the root principles of Protestantism. I should ask this question:

[1]*An American Dialogue* (New York: Doubleday, 1960), p. 189.

Why was it that for more than 200 years the Protestants had no interest in "the missions"? Dr. K.S. Latourette, in his monumental *History of the Expansion of Christianity* (Vol. III, pp. 25-54), develops six reasons to account for "the greater prominence of Roman Catholics as against Protestants in the propagation of Christianity" during this period. These reasons are of great interest; but to discuss them would carry us too far afield. Yet I venture a conjecture about the root outlook of "Protestantism." I do not think that the root difference between Catholicism and Protestantism concerns the way in which man attains to God and expresses his relationship with God; nor what man can do without God; nor is it what God does when he "justifies" man. Rather, it is *what men can, under God, do for one another.* Here lies the reason for the rejection of indulgences, of the sacrifice of the Mass, of the "other five sacraments," especially the sacrament of Penance, of prayers for the dead, invocation of saints and especially of our Lady, of the authority of the Church and, in general, of the whole *corporate* system of Catholicism. I do not think that the difference between Luther and Catholics about the sacrifice of the Mass turned on any abstract questions or assumptions about sacrifice demanding a death, real or mystic; I think it turned on the question *whether a Mass could do good to others than those present at it.* And in that question is concentrated the whole issue, namely, in what sense is Christ's salvation meant to be "individual," in what sense "corporate" or "collective."

If this is correct—and I think there is much to be said for it—then the ecumenical movement, with its interest in collectivity and its interest in a corporate expression of Christianity, is a more radical revision of Protestantism than ecumenists themselves realize.

However that may be, I draw two conclusions:

a. Protestants, I think, are apt to be less led by logic and more by feeling than are Catholics. The completely logical system of Catholic theology makes small appeal to many Protestants, who still consciously or unconsciously are led by "the experience of conversion," by hymns and by sermons which appeal to the feelings. It has been said that what corresponds to moral, physical and metaphysical certitude in Anglicanism is as follows: Moral certitude is expressed by "May it not be?"; and metaphysical certitude by "I do feel."

b. Protestants are more affected by signs of good will and of kindness than are Catholics—partly, perhaps because they have not the inner security of Catholics, partly because they are led more by feeling than are Catholics. I have found that expression of a theological difference tends to be regarded as a sign of ill will—however much they may proclaim that they want frankness and candor. And contrarywise, I have been several times astonished at the effect produced by an effort to appreciate their writers or administrators.

Here I should agree that there is a problem: If we are very kind and mild, do we thereby tend to encourage them in their errors? Is not a somewhat uncompromising and immediate advance to the root of the differences between us the most charitable, even though painful at first method of procedure?

I remember asking an ex-Anglican who had been an Anglican nun, what brought her into the Church. She laughed and said:

"It was the rudeness of one of your priests, Father."

"How so?"

"Well, I used to pass this priest on the street, and one day he stopped me and asked what convent I came from. I told him St. Catherine's. He looked puzzled and I explained that it was an Anglican convent.

" 'Ah, shure, now,' said he, 'and you're not a nun at all.'

" 'What do you mean,' I answered, 'of course I am a nun, with the same vows that Catholic nuns have. And we keep our rules well, let me tell you that.'

" 'Ah,' said he, 'and who has authority to take your vows?' "

The good lady told me she went away furious at what she regarded as ignorant rudeness and lack of charity. But the question remained in her mind—with the ultimate result that she became a Catholic, though only after some years. Shock tactics may sometimes be best, but not generally, I think.

The mind of the Holy Father

In answer to this question the Holy Father has given a clear indication of his mind.

In the issue of February 1st, 1959, the editor of the *Osservatore Romano* gave the substance of an address by the Pope: "The faults of which Catholics are not, alas, free, lie in our not having prayed enough to God to smooth the ways that converge on Christ's Church; in not having felt charity to the full; in not having always practiced it towards our separated brethren, preferring the rigor of learned, logical, incontrovertible arguments to forbearing and patient love which has its own compelling power of persuasion; in having preferred the philosophical rigidity of the lecture-room to the friendly serenity of the *Controversie* of St. Francis of Sales."

The *Herder-Korrespondenz* in March 1959 quoted the Holy Father as having said:

"We do not intend to conduct a trial of the past; we do not want to prove who was right or who was wrong. All we want to say is: 'Let us come together. Let us make an end of our divisions.'"

In June 1959 an Anglican, Canon Rea, reported that the Holy Father had said to him: "In working for reunion, it is necessary first to be very meek and humble, secondly, to be patient and know how to await God's hour, and thirdly, to avoid discussions that may hurt the virtue of charity, leaving aside for the moment those elements on which we differ."

On the 7th of May, 1960, "at the close of his address" to missionaries, "the Holy Father appealed for a real understanding of those brethren who, while bearing the name of Christ on their foreheads and indeed in their hearts, are yet separated from the Catholic Church. We must bestir ourselves and not rest until we have overcome our old habits of thought, our prejudices and the use of expressions that are anything but courteous, so as to create a climate favorable to the reconciliations we look forward to, and so in every way to co-operate with the work of grace. Thus to one and all will be thrown wide open the gates to the unity of the Church of our Lord and Savior Jesus Christ" (*Osservatore,* May 11, 1960).

The setting up of the Secretariat for Promoting the Unity of Christians, in preparation for the Second Vatican Council, in the words of the Holy Father, is "a token of our affection and good will towards those who bear the name of Christian but yet are separated from the Apostolic see."

The emotional factors

The Holy Father appears to have a true insight into the situation at present. Loyalty to "Protestantism" seems to me to be in the order of emotion, not in the order of intellect. Consequently it must be dealt with in the emotional order as well as in the intellectual order. The image of Catholicism which has been built up over centuries—by history, by literature, poetry, songs and hymns, by family and national associations, by inherited prejudices and associations—cannot be changed by rational arguments alone, though certainly these play their part. The image of the Pope has become an image of a tyrant, or of a good man enmeshed in a net of Italian intrigue. This image must be changed. The Holy Father is the center of the authority of the Church, of the jurisdiction, of the doctrinal unity: this is known and understood—and rejected. The Holy Father is also the center of the charity of the Church: as St. Irenaeus said, president in love, president of love. This image must displace the image of the tyrant who restricts or suppresses legitimate freedom.

I think that it is largely due to this emotional factor that Catholic theological books are rarely read by Protestants, and then the books selected are often French or German. There may be, of course, various reasons for this failure to consider Catholic writings: possibly we write in an idiom strange to them, possibly they feel that our presuppositions are so alien that not much can be learned from us, and possibly they mistrust our objectivity, feeling that a Catholic has his conclusions before he begins to investigate and write. The fact, however, is a fact, and presents a challenge to us.

b. *The effort to obtain a* consensus *about the nature of the Church*

The modern search for a consensus may be said to have begun in 1910 at the Edinburgh Missionary Conference, although many different efforts had previously been made, none of which assumed permanent form. Protestant missionary organizations had become acutely aware that the divisions among Christians were a serious obstacle to the expansion of Christianity among non-Christians. This Conference of 1910 formed a "continuation committee" which resulted in the International Missionary Council, whose main function was the negotiation of "comity agreements," that is agreements among missionary organizations which lessened if they did not prevent competition between them in non-Christian lands. The 1914 war came as a shock to many sincere Christians, and resulted in various efforts to apply Christian principles to international, and then, also, to economic and social relations. The outcome was the Life and Work movement, which avoided doctrinal issues and urged co-operation on the practical level. Service, they said, unites, doctrine divides.

By 1927, however, many were convinced that the doctrinal issues could not and indeed should not be avoided. From this conviction sprang the Lausanne Conference on Faith and Order of 1927, and the Edinburgh Conference on Faith and Order of 1937.

Search for formulas

At this period, there was a general tendency to seek for formulas which would express a general agreement among Christians, even though behind the formula lay radical disagreements. At the time this was either not recognized or not admitted. And, as even now, the justice of Pius XI's insistence on the need of firm doctrinal foundations in his Encyclical *Mortalium Animos* is only tardily being recognized. As the tendencies towards a certain "latitudinarianism" are not wholly eradicated, a citation from the recent biography of Arthud Cayley Headlam, Anglican Bishop of Gloucester (1923-1945, died 1947) may be pertinent:

"A dominating feature of his work was his insistence that agreement on broad principles was all that was necessary for reunion; agreement on details or on the interpretation of the fundamentals of faith and order were not necessary. Many scholars have considered this to be a mistake; and admittedly it has produced difficulties. Here is the judgment of the Russian theologian, Professor N. Arseniev: 'His great gift, his great instrument wherewith to serve the Church of God was his scholarship and his fine power of organization and of uniting intellectual efforts of different people for a great common work. He found admirable well-adapted words to summarize the opinions of others, to propose a common formula, an intellectual bridge. And here perhaps was a weak point of his: his love for synthetical unifying formulae, for conciliatory overbridging of differences, that were sometimes premature and could sometimes conceal the deeper issues behind them. But how clear-cut, how lucid was his interpretation of the problem and of the different approaches thereto, and how he knew and respected the spiritual independence of others. This made him an ideal chairman, full of lucidity, of sense for order and of tolerance.' It was, of course, a fact that he was an admirable chairman of conferences on reunion. By virtue of long experience he knew exactly what procedure to adopt, how to treat the issues, and what resolutions a conference was likely to accept. But his too liberal approach could lead to inconsistencies. To assure both Orthodox and Lutheran theologians, for example, that the Church of England was in general agreement with their respective views on Confirmation, when both those Churches did not themselves agree, solved nothing. It bred doubt. It certainly bred doubt in the minds of some of the more rigid Orthodox theologians. 'If he is so inconsistent, how can we trust him?' some of them asked.

"But to Headlam there was no real inconsistency. He was doggedly determined to follow a policy: it may have appeared a rather rough and ready policy to some, but it was a policy inspired by a vision. 'A Church which produced Clement of Alexandria and Origen, Athanasius and the Alexandrine school, Chrysostom and the Antiochene school, the great Cappadocians, the two Gregories and Bais, the African school, Tertullian, Cyprian, Augustine, Leo and Gregory the Great, shows no narrowness and no failure in spiritual power. It conquered the ancient world; it subdued the untrained vigour of the barbarians. A Church which was based not on confession but on such a tradition would embrace in its fold evangelists and those we wrongly call Catholics, modernists and pietists, Lutherans and Calvinists. There would be a home in it for all that is true in Romanism or Orthodoxy or Anglicanism. It would be a free home for the working of the spirit.' "[2]

Headlam's outlook was undoubtedly shared by many ecumenists in the twenties and even the thirties. The Edinburgh Conference on Faith and Order, however, showed that the differences were more profound than Headlam's point of view recognized, and showed that practically every theological question came back to the fundamental question of the nature of the Church. After Edinburgh, there was a greater resolve to face the difficulties squarely; and in preparation for the Conference of Amsterdam of 1948, an attempt was made to focus the differences as between what was called "a catholic outlook" and "a protestant outlook"—a division which undoubtedly was much influenced by the production of *Catholicity* in 1947 by an exceedingly able group of Anglo-Catholics, among whom were Gregory Dix, Lionel Thornton, and the present Archbishop of Canterbury, Arthur Michael Ramsey. At Amsterdam, however, the administrative questions involved in forming the World Council assumed greater importance than the doctrinal. In preparation for the Lund Conference of Faith and Order in 1952, an attempt was made to list all agreements and differences in convictions about the nature of the Church, and there was considerable insistence that the differences should be faced as frankly as the agreements. At Lund in 1952 these differences were listed as carefully as possible.

The headings were as follows:

1. The Limits of the Church and its Mode of Definition.
2. The Continuity of the Church.
3. The Unity of the Church.
4. The Goal of the Reunion Movement.
5. The Number and Nature of the Sacraments and their Relation to Membership in the Church.

[2]Ronald Jasper, *Arthur Cayley Headlam, the Life and Letters of a Bishop* (London, 1960), p. 361-362.

6. Scripture and Tradition.
7. Infallibility.
8. Priesthood and Sacrifice.

As a result of the discussions two convictions emerged, which have been the general principles on which the World Council of Churches has acted ever since:

1. There must be an effort to go behind the differences to more universal principles of agreement; the mere listing of agreements and disagreements produces a stalemate.

Part of the reason for this conclusion lay in the perception that differences apparently small in themselves involved difference of total system. Instances of this may be found in the Anglo-Catholic view of Confirmation by a bishop, in the Congregationalist view on occasional lay celebration of the Eucharist and in the Baptist view of believer's baptism.

After Lund, in 1952, four main subjects were selected for studies by groups of theologians from different "traditions": Christ and the Church; Tradition and Traditions; Ways of Worship; and Institutionalism. At Evanston in 1954, the Faith and Order Commission was made part of the Division of Studies in the World Council—a development which needs further discussion.

2. Theological discussion by itself is not enough: there must be some kind of "cross-fertilization" between churches, some kind of living together. Concretely, this means more formal recognition given to what is called "Inter-church Aid and Service to Refugees" and indirectly, the whole of the modern missionary problem. Together with this goes the Commission of the Churches for International Affairs; the Department for Co-operation of men and women; the place of lay men and women in the church, and a number of other matters, such as surveys of human needs in under-developed countries; youth work of diverse kinds, and, speaking generally, an effort to form what may be called a theoretical and a practical Christian sociology, taking the word sociology in the broadest sense.

This is an aspect of the work of the World Council of Churches which I confess I did not understand or appreciate for a long time: the problem seemed to me to be almost exclusively doctrinal and these other activities seemed to me to be a distraction from the main issue, and even something in the nature of a narcotic, since they satisfy the desire to do something without coming to grips with the radical causes of division. It took me long to realize that the divisions among Protestants, and among the Orthodox (since it is a mistake to think that the Orthodox are perfectly united), lie largely in the emotional order, and that involvement in common charitable work is a unifying factor, which tends to dissolve prejudices and to open minds to wider perspectives; doctrinal agreement cannot be attained exclusively in the study or in the conference room, but is the fruit of common feeling as well as of common thinking.

These non-doctrinal activities, too, help to a wider spread of the ecumenical idea, for within the World Council the most recent development has been the recognition that the insights and agreements among the leaders have not percolated down to the ordinary ministers and still less to the man in the pew.

Concurrently with these developments in the World Council has gone a considerable number of mergers or reunions between churches of the same tradition, such as unions of differing bodies of Presbyterians, Methodists and Lutherans,[3] and also between churches of different traditions, such as the Church of South India formed by a coalescence of Anglicans, Congregationalists, Methodists and Presbyterians, and the United Church of Christ in the United States. At the present moment over one hundred independent church bodies are engaged in negotiations for mergers or unions.

Parallel with this development towards amalgamation of churches, go two other developments: the formation of re-

---

[3]The term, v.g. Lutheran does not designate a church; in the U.S.A. some independent Lutheran bodies can be named: The Lutheran Church in the United States, the American Lutheran Church, the United Lutheran Church, the Augustana Lutheran Church, the Lutheran Church–Missouri Synod, the Evangelical Lutheran Church, the Lutheran Free Church. It must be admitted that part of the reason for these divisions among Lutherans in the United States lies in the different countries of origin from which their members sprang. Language and nationality are a potent cause of division, even in Catholic dioceses, as no doubt you are better aware than I am.

gional, national and local councils, and the rise of denominational world alliances or federations, such as the Lutheran World Federation, the Presbyterian World Alliance, the Baptist World Conference and similar groupings.

The regional councils embrace representatives of churches in different nations, v.g. the East Asian Christian Conference, the Near East Christian Council, in which some Orthodox participate. Here might be mentioned the Committee for Co-operation in Latin America, which is a sub-division of the Missionary branch of the National Council of Churches of Christ in the U.S.A. National Councils vary in strength of numbers and in effectiveness: usually they distribute World Council literature and foster prayer for unity in January.

The influence of the world denominational associations, or alliances, or federation, is as yet not clear. One of the most active is the Lutheran World Federation which publishes in English and German *The Lutheran World*, which gives much information about ecumenism and has useful bibliographies. The Baptist world conference is of interest since it includes Baptists within the World Council of Churches, such as the American Baptist Convention, and the English Baptist Union, as well as Baptist groups which stand aloof from the World Council, such as the Southern Baptist Convention and the Regular Baptists of America.

Thus, the effort to overcome the fissiparous tendency of Protestantism—which exists, though to a lesser extent, among the Orthodox—is proceeding in different ways. It should be noted that these efforts are on a world-wide scale, and that the problems involved in divided Christendom are more and more being recognized as global problems. There are many reasons for this. In the modern age, technological and sociological developments are bringing changes throughout the whole world. Newsprint and literature, radio, television and films, rapid travel by aeroplane: all these spread ideas and profoundly influence the patterns of community, home and individual life. Moreover, the attainment of political independence by many countries brings demands for ecclesiastical independence, and occasionally for excessive integration of national and religious culture. This has raised many problems for non-Catholic missionary agencies which give support to churches in lands recently become independent. The demand not seldom is for administrative independence, even where local resources do not permit financial independence: to put it bluntly, money is welcome but control disliked; and there is denial of the adage, "he who pays the piper calls the tune." In some of the "unions" or mergers proposed, finance is involved since funds have been left to religious bodies with doctrinal conditions, v.g. retention of the doctrine of the Synod of Dort. Thus there is a close connection, in the concrete, between doctrine, administration, and relationships with missionary boards which support Christianity abroad. These problems have become more manifestly global, for what is done in one country is quickly cited as a reason why it should be done in another. Here lies one reason for the "integration" of the International Missionary Council and the World Council of Churches.

A Crisis in the World Council?

For the last five or six years the Faith and Order Commission of the World Council of Churches has shown some dissatisfaction with its position in the organizational set-up: some declared that it was being overlaid by the many other activities of the World Council of Churches, and that doctrinal issues were being submerged by the practical co-operation in charitable works undertaken by the Council. This is evident from the last four Reports of its annual meetings. It seemed to many that concern for doctrinal unity was lessening and that the Faith and Order Commision did not hold the place of importance which it merits.

Originally, the Faith and Order grouping was quite independent of any other organization, notably of the Life and Work movement and of the International Missionary Council. When in 1948 the World Council of Churches was formed, the Faith and Order Commission remained independent, but its status was not defined. In 1954 after Evanston it was made part of the Division of Studies, within which are also the Sections dealing with Evangelism, Church and Society and Missionary Studies. This seemed to reduce its standing in the organization of the Council. Further, the theological Commissions which, within Faith and Order, studied various matters, proceeded slowly and have not even yet produced their final Reports. The Secretary of Faith and Order was not necessarily a member of the Central Committee of the Council. Consequently, a feeling grew up that on the one hand the theologians were "going round in circles" and not advancing much, and, on the other, that the relative importance of Faith and Order was lessened, especially in popular estimation, by its subordinate position in the organizational set-up of the World Council.

From 1956 onwards, the members of the Faith and Order Commission,[4] or, rather, their leaders, began to urge:

1. That Faith and Order should be made a Division.
2. That it should have a larger Staff, and a larger budget.
3. That its Director should be an important official in the Central Committee.
4. That it should take more part in church union negotiations.

---

[4]J. Robert Nelson (American Methodist) former Secretary of Faith and Order, Oliver Tomkins (Anglican Bishop of Bristol), Keith Bridston (American Lutheran, present Secretary of the Faith and Order Commission), Leslie Newbigin (Bishop in the Church of South India), Douglas Horton (United Church of Christ, emeritus Dean of Harvard Theological School), Henri D'Espine (Swiss Reformed), John Marsh (English Congregationalist), R.R. Hartford (Irish Anglican), Vernon Bartlett (Quaker), Edmund Schlink (German Lutheran), W.A. Norgren (present Secretary of Faith and Order Department of American Council of Churches), J.R. Chandran (Church of South India), Georges Florovsky (Russian exile Orthodox, at Harvard), G.F. Wingren (Church of Sweden),—and others, such as Eugene Fairweather and David W. Hay, both of Canada, Clifford Moorhouse, of the Episcopal Church in America, K.E. Skydsgaard of Denmark, Bishop Timiadis (Orthodox on the Staff at Geneva); Archbishop A. Michael Ramsey of York, G.R. Cragg, of United Church of Canada, Pier Edwall of Sweden, Bishop Lilje of Germany (East), Paul Minear of United Church of Christ USA, Anders Nygren, Bishop in Sweden, Thomas Torrance of The Church of Scotland, Seppo Teinonen, of Finland, Robert Tobias, Disciple of Christ, USA., Alan Watson, Australian Presbyterian, L.B. Champion, English Baptist, and several others (this list is by no means complete).

5. That it should hold world Conferences on Faith and Order, apart from meetings of the Assembly.

6. In general that there should be greater recognition of the importance of the Faith and Order issues and of their urgency.

7. That the definition of the goal of the movement which the Commission had drawn up should be sent to the Churches for their consideration and acceptance.

The definition of the goal of the movement is possibly the most important doctrinal statement made during the last ten years. It occurs in the Report on the Future of Faith and Order and reads as follows:

"The Faith and Order movement was born in the hope that it would be, under God, a help to the churches in realizing His will for the unity of the Church. The formation of the World Council of Churches, and the incorporation of Faith and Order in it, have changed the circumstances under which Faith and Order works, but have not changed its purpose. We have become convinced that the time has come for a fuller statement of this purpose, and for a re-examination of the means by which Faith and Order should, within the World Council of Churches, seek its realization.

"The Commission on Faith and Order understands that the unity which is both God's will and His gift to His Church is one which brings all in each place[5] who confess Christ Jesus as Lord into a fully committed fellowship with one another through one baptism into Him, holding the one apostolic faith, preaching the one Gospel and breaking the one bread, and having a corporate life reaching out in witness and service to all; and which at the same time unites them with the whole Christian fellowship in all places and all ages in such wise that ministry and members are acknowledged by all, and that all can act and speak together as occasion requires for the tasks to which God calls the Church.

[5]The word "place" here is used both in its primary sense of local neighborhood and also, under more modern conditions, of other areas in which Christians need to express unity in Christ, e.g. all those engaged in a local industry.

"It is for such unity that we believe we must pray and work. Such a vision has indeed been the inspiration of the Faith and Order movement in the past, and we re-affirm that this is still our goal. We recognize that the brief definition of our objective which we have given above leaves many questions unanswered. In particular we would state emphatically that the unity we seek is not one of uniformity, nor a monolithic power structure, and that on the interpretation and the means of achieving certain of the matters specified in the preceding paragraph we are not yet of a common mind. The achievement of unity will involve nothing less than a death and rebirth for many forms of church life as we have known them. We believe that nothing less costly can finally suffice."

To a Catholic that definition may sound rather roundabout and very abstract. It must, however, be read in the light of the actual doctrines about the Church held by many Protestants, especially by the large mass of Protestants who are under the impression that Christianity consists mainly in two things: 1) Self-committal to Christ as revealed in the New Testament; and 2) the performance of some actual works of charity, v.g. support of missions, of the poor, of orphans, etc. This is apt to be the ordinary man's interpretation of the general doctrine of "justification by faith alone."

However, to return to the definition of the goal of the movement, which I have just given, the following should be carefully noted:

1. The need for unity at the *local level* is stressed. By this is meant that there ought not to be a number of "churches" in one town or neighborhood. The idea of people belonging to a denomination is rejected, v.g. no one should be able to say: "I am an Anglican," "I am a Baptist," "I am a Congregationalist, or a Methodist, or a Lutheran, or a Presbyterian." All ought to say: "We belong to the one holy catholic apostolic Church."

2. A merely *invisible* unity is rejected. Clearly "a corporate life reaching out in witness and service to all," the being able "to speak together," and the acknowledgement of members and ministry by all, demands a visible unity in the order of organization.

In this is rejected the idea of a "federation" of churches,

such as is the World Council itself, or such as is the Lutheran World Federation, or mergers or amalgamations short of organic unity.

3. The unity aimed at is said to be such as is continuous with all Christians throughout history: "unites them with the whole Christian fellowship in all places *and all ages.*" This implicitly denies the too common Protestant idea that the sole norm is the Christianity of apostolic times, and that in intervening ages the Church was so corrupt that it practically ceased to be until the reforms of the sixteenth century.

4. *Unity in faith* is stressed by the double reference: "holding the one apostolic faith" and "preaching the one Gospel." In fact, the words "holding the one apostolic faith" were a later insertion at the suggestion of the Lutherans, who felt that the term "preaching the one Gospel" did not define clearly enough the need to have the same faith as the Apostles and feared lest perhaps "the one Gospel" might be understood in the purely "evangelical" sense that "we are saved by Jesus Christ" and that this message of salvation is the full content of the faith.[6]

5. The term "breaking the one bread" although it leaves the doctrine of the *Eucharist* vague, nevertheless in its reference to 1 Cor. 10:16–19 is worthy noting. "The cup of blessing that we bless, is it not the sharing of the blood of Christ? And the bread we break, is it not the partaking of the body of the Lord? Because the bread is one, we though many, are

[6]I think that the vast majority of member churches of the World Council of Churches would recite both the Apostles' Creed and the Nicene Creed, with the exception of the Disciples of Christ, who have traditionally an aversion to any formulation of faith other than the New Testament. It is not that they do not hold all the doctrines of these two creeds, but that (being founded by Alexander Campbell who was disgusted with the disputes in the nineteenth century among Scotch Presbyterians divided into seven parties, and therefore rejected all formulations of faith) they traditionally are averse to any formulation. Some others might conceivably say that the *homoousios,* consubstantial, of Nicaea is too influenced by Greek philosophy and is today a needless complication; and the Orthodox, of course, would reject the *Filioque.* It is worth noting that many of the Disciples of Christ tend to be "fundamentalist" and to insist on adult baptism.

one body, all of us who partake of the one bread. Behold Israel according to the flesh, are not they who eat of the sacrifices partakers of the altar?"

The second part of the definition of the goal of the movement admits that "many questions are left unanswered"; and this is almost a needless observation. For instance, what is the nature of the ministry which must be acknowledged by all? Through what medium are all to be able "to speak together"?

The rejection of "uniformity" and of "a monolithic power structure" caused me to wonder whether the Catholic Church is implicitly referred to. I asked one of those closely associated with Faith and Order if the Catholic Church was regarded as imposing "uniformity" and as being "a monolithic power structure." He answered that possibly some did regard the Catholic Church in this way, but gave two reasons why this need not be the exclusive meaning: first, that some Churches demand very great uniformity in ritual, v.g. prescribing the exact number of hymns to be sung at each service and the exact hymn book to be used; some forbid anything in the nature of "free prayer," (i.e. prayers not written down) which the Congregationalists like and practice; and some forbid any advance into new liturgical forms. The other reason he gave was the fear expressed by many inside the World Council, and repeated incessantly by non-cooperating bodies, that the World Council is aiming at becoming "a Super-Church." Dr. W. A. Visser 't Hooft wrote an article on this subject in the *Ecumenical Review*, July, 1958, the burden of which was to deny that the World Council was trying to become "a centralized ecclesiastical institution of world-wide character which seeks to impose unity and uniformity by means of outward pressure and political influence," or "a centralized, authoritarian, monopolistic and politically minded ecclesiastical system." Doubtless these repudiations do represent what some non-Catholics imagine the Catholic Church to be; but the mere repudiations do not certainly imply acceptance of those descriptions as true of the Catholic Church.

The theological Commission preparatory to Lund which discussed the theological assumptions of the World Council (the Commission's report was entitled *The Church*, edited by Newton Flew) made a remark which is too often overlooked:

"It is essential to distinguish sharply between what the Council says about the Council and what it says about the Church. For example, the statement (Official Report of the Lund Conference, p. 127) that 'the Council disavows any thought of becoming a single unified church structure' refers to the Council, and leaves entirely open whether the Church should ever be 'dominated by a centralized administrative authority.'"

Similarly, it is essential to distinguish sharply between what individual theologians on the World Council believe as individuals or as members of their own Church, and what is expressed in the official documents drawn up in their Conferences.

This particular document, defining the aim of the Faith and Order Commission does, indeed, leave many questions unanswered; nevertheless, as far as it goes there is nothing in it contrary to Catholic teaching, there is much that Catholics can wholeheartedly accept, and Catholics can hold that the definition as a whole can only be actualized by accepting the Catholic position. All that is said of the Church is in fact realized in the Catholic Church. But to convince Protestants and the Orthodox of this is our problem.

Notable are the words:

"The achievement of unity will involve nothing less than a death and rebirth for many forms of Church life as we have known them."

A sense of urgency was plain. The comment on the first function of the Faith and Order Commission reads as follows:

"To proclaim the essential oneness of the Church of Christ and to keep prominently before the World Council and the Churches the obligation to manifest that unity and its urgency for the work of evangelism.

"It is our strong conviction that to proclaim the essential oneness of the Church of Christ involves facing the question 'what kind of unity does God demand of His Church?' We agree that no one definition of the nature of unity can be a condition of membership in the World Council of Churches, but Faith and Order exists in order to stand for the unity of the Church as the will of God and for a ceaseless effort to know what obedience to that will means concretely. Only so can it be 'manifest.' The World Council of Churches can have no 'neutrality' on whether that question is answered or not. Clearly the World Council is not in a position to say what the answer is in all its fullness; if it were, our quest for the 'manifest unity' would already be at an end. As the Toronto Statement of 1950 put it: 'As the conversation between the Churches develops, and as the Churches enter into closer contact with each other, they will no doubt have to face new decisions and problems. For the Council exists to break the deadlock between the Churches' (*ibid.*, V.2.) *All* the churches in the Council confront each other under the demand of God Himself that they should learn from Him the nature of the unity which we seek. It has been characteristic of Faith and Order to recognize that patience and thoroughness are needed for this task. But it is also necessary to recognize that in such matters we are not entirely free to proceed at our own pace, that events are forcing upon us various kinds of Christian co-operation, and that if we do not find true unity we shall find ourselves remaining content with a form of organizational unity which leaves unfulfilled many of the central requirements of the Church's life. There is therefore need for a proper sense of urgency lest we lose the time that God gives us. Faith and Order must constantly press upon the Council and the churches the fact that the question of unity is one upon which an answer has to be given, and that to give no answer means to be shut up to the wrong answer. Specifically, Faith and Order must raise this question:

a. in Assemblies so far as its programme for the whole World Council of Churches allows;

b. in Central Committee from time to time as best serves, as well as in the Theological Commissions which all at least bear upon the answer.

All these are ways in which Faith and Order makes its witness within the World Council of Churches, but in order ultimately to reach the churches themselves, for whose sake all this activity is organized."

The theological implications of the World Council cause

much discussion. Two interpretations of the actual state of the World Council are prominent:

a. The World Council of Churches is becoming an agency for academic study and for co-operation in good works, including fostering missions. This interpretation lays emphasis upon the affirmation made at Toronto in 1950 that "no Church is obliged to change its ecclesiology as a consequence of membership in the World Council."

b. The World Council of Churches is becoming a Super-Church, that is, a bureaucratic institution which lessens the independence of the member Churches. This interpretation lays emphasis on the Toronto affirmation that "the Council exists in order to break the deadlock between the Churches."

According to the emphasis laid on one or the other of these conceptions, different practical conclusions are drawn: a) that the Churches should not do separately what it is possible for them to do together; and b) that the Churches should do separately everything that is possible and do together only what is necessary for efficiency.

However, there is no theoretical solution to the problems involved in these different emphases. I must confess that I thought the Report on the Future of Faith and Order was perhaps too strong medicine to be taken by churches of a "congregationalist" polity; but at St. Andrews in 1960 the Report was accepted unanimously by both the Faith and Order Commission and by the Central Committee. It was presented for general acceptance by the Churches at the Assembly in New Delhi, November-December, 1961.

As a result of the St. Andrews meeting in August 1960, the Faith and Order Commission obtained more men, more money, more Conferences, both regional and a World Conference planned for 1963, more dissemination of its insights and a stronger position on the World Council for its Director.

Before leaving the subject, a word on the matter of the week of prayer for unity.

The Sub-Committee of Faith and Order on Regional and National Developments said this about the Week of Prayer for Christian Unity:

"We are convinced that the work of Faith and Order will

find its foundation in prayer. Therefore the committee suggests:

a. that the Week of Prayer for Christian Unity be provided with additional popular and promotional literature where appropriate.

b. that interconfessional Bible study be undertaken in connection with this Week.

c. that ecumenical retreats and schools of prayer might be features of this Week.

d. that all material for the observance be made available not later than half a year before, so that adequate promotion can take place."

c. *An openness to Catholic insights*

1. *At the official level,* the door to cooperation with the Catholic Church has always been kept open, in spite of the prejudice of some members of the World Council of Churches (on this cf. Oliver Tomkins' account in Rouse & Neill, *History of the Ecumenical Movement*). In no official document does anything occur which would be offensive to Catholics.

2. Two *recent official statements* may be quoted.

The Faith and Order Report of 1960 says this:

"*Relations with Christians outside the World Council of Churches membership:*

"One of our basic principles is to draw churches out of isolation into conference. In this connection, we believe that we have a responsibility, in this time in which our member churches have been able to overcome that isolation by meeting in the World Council of Churches, especially towards those churches which have chosen not to avail themselves of that particular opportunity. We also note that we are empowered to invite representatives of such churches to serve in our Commission (v. Constitution, para. 5 (II) b), and so, by implication, on our Theological Commissions.

"We have especially in mind two groups among those who 'accept Our Lord Jesus Christ as God and Saviour.'

"a. *The Roman Catholic Church* constitutes so large a part of Christendom that we are bound to take it into consideration in our work for Christian unity. But we realize the very serious difficulties which arise, both from their side and from ours, to hinder any official or clearly defined relationship. Yet Faith and Order is an aspect of the World Council of Churches in which the Roman Catholic Church has shown an interest. Roman Catholic theologians have made important contributions by their writings to the discussion of Faith and Order issues. We believe that this theological discussion should be pursued in whatever ways may be mutually acceptable.

"b. *Protestant churches* outside the World Council of Churches need another form of approach, for as compared with the unity (though complex) of the Roman Catholic Church, we are here dealing with very diverse entities. But we believe that many of them are ready to enter into common study with the World Council of Churches and to meet in personal contact in various countries and regions. They comprise another group of fellow-Christians with whom Faith and Order should enter into fellowship on the ground of common concern for Christian mission and unity.

"With regard to them both, we would urge that Faith and Order should:

"I. aim at a situation in the World Council of Churches staff which ensured that there should always be people sufficiently free from other commitments to make it a first charge on their time to be in continuous, personal and well-informed contact with the whole complexity of both these groups;

"II. on the basis of such contact, the Faith and Order Secretariat, Working Committee and other groups in Faith and Order would be in a position to be kept informed of developments and openings, and so able to seek their participation in our theological work where it was then deemed possible and advisable."

Is there any inconsistency in seeking contacts with the Catholic Church on the one hand, and bodies like the Southern Baptist Convention and the Pentecostalists on the other?

There is no inconsistency. The World Council of Churches is an organization which tries to unite all those who "accept Jesus Christ as the Lord and Saviour and therefore endeavour to fulfil their common purpose to the glory of the one God,

Father, Son and Holy Spirit." It is a *council*, that is, a meeting place in which Christians seek to overcome divisions and to unite in the one holy catholic apostolic Church founded by Jesus Christ. None who accept the basis of Christological and Trinitarian belief can be excluded; but beyond this basis, there are no ecclesiological assumptions.

In fact, however, I have reason to think that there is far more inclination towards the Catholic Church than towards any other non-member Christian body. Catholic theologians in Germany, Belgium, France, Spain, Rome, England and the United States have followed the ecumenical movement with intense interest. Books and periodicals—*Una Sancta, Istina, Vers l'unité chrétienne, Irenikon, Unitas,* and *The Heythrop Journal*—have followed the movement with discriminating sympathy. Sometimes the sympathy has been more evident than the discrimination, and sometimes the discrimination more evident than the sympathy. But on the whole I think it is true to say that Catholics have shown far more helpful interest than non-cooperating Protestants. The writings of Catholics have been read with assiduity by leaders of the World Council of Churches, and have not been without effect. I have heard it said on good authority that Dr. W. S. Visser 't Hooft used to read all Catholic comments, until recently when he found that too much was written by Catholics for him to be able to follow it all.

3. The four Theological Commissions of Faith and Order produced "interim reports" in 1960: on Christ and the Church, on Tradition and Traditions, on Ways of Worship, and on "Institutionalism." Only the Report on Christ and the Church has been published, under the title *One Lord, One Baptism* (S C M Press, London, 1960[7]). In an appendix I copy the list of the four Commissions on Faith and Order.

Noteworthy in this Report is the insistence that the doctrine of Christ and the Church derives from the doctrine of the Trinity, and the insistence on the doctrine of Nicaea and of Chalcedon for understanding the union of Christ and the Church. This Report also considered the question of Baptism, and it

---

[7]American edition published in 1961 by Augsburg Publishing House, Minneapolis.

insisted that the effect of the sacrament is participation at once in Christ in his redeeming work and in the Church which is Christ's body. Two questions, however, were left unsettled: that of infant baptism as against believers' baptism, and the relation between baptism and confirmation. A principle of solution, however, was indicated: that the act of baptizing is a representative act of the whole Church; but the implications of this were not fully developed.

The Reports on *Tradition and Traditions* were produced, in the European section, mainly by Professor K. E. Skydsgaard of Copenhagen, and in the North American section by Professor Jaroslav Pelikan, under the title *Overcoming History by History.* Both these papers took the position that scripture alone cannot be the norm of faith, giving the usual reasons alleged by Catholics. This subject seems to me to be both the most fundamental and the one in which most progress, to some extent under Orthodox influence, has been made towards the Catholic position. As yet, however, the question has not been faced how to distinguish what is a true tradition from a false one, and the discussions remain somewhat abstract, and the question of the development of doctrine has not been faced.

Nevertheless, the following words of Dr. Eugene Carson Blake, Stated Clerk of the United Presbyterian Church of the United States of America, in proposing a union of his Church with the Protestant Episcopalians, the Methodists and the United Church of Christ, imply that the Church under the guidance of the Holy Spirit, is judge both of Tradition and of the interpretation of scripture:

"The reformation Churches have traditionally grounded their authority for faith and life on the Scriptures alone. So long as the wording 'Sole Scriptura' is required, no bridge can be made between catholic and evangelical. But it is now clear in ecumenical conversations that Protestants generally have come to recognize the right place of tradition, just as Catholics have generally become aware of the rightness of judging all tradition by the Scriptures as interpreted for the Church by the Holy Spirit."

In passing, I add some of the questions on which Tradition

seems most important and on which Scripture alone is not a satisfactory norm; in theological dialogue these questions will, I venture to think, assume greater importance.

1. Most conspicuous: *infant baptism.* This question is far more ramifying than sometimes appears: Augustine used it as a proof of original sin: *in remissionem peccatorum,* against Pelagius *and* as a proof of the absolute gratuity of grace against the semi-Pelagians.

2. Heretics can baptize validly and fruitfully: Stephen against Cyprian: *nihil innovatur nisi quod traditum est, ut manus eis imponatur in paenitentiam.*

3. The rejection of Donatism: that baptism must not be repeated even though received in bad dispositions, v.g. by hypocrites from hypocrites.

Consequent upon this: what is the gift infallibly received in any "valid" baptism?

4. Canon of Scripture: v.g. the rejection of the Shepherd of Hermas, and the question of the Deutero-canonical books of the Old Testament.

5. The penitential discipline and annexed questions.

6. Mary "ever virgin": Mary the second Eve as Christ the second Adam; Mary theotokos.

7. Invocation of saints.

8. Prayers for the dead.

9. Special gift of the Holy Spirit received after Baptism: the whole matter of "confirmation."

10. Christ the principal minister in sacraments: Judas baptizat, Christus baptizat.

11. One city, one episcopos—Ignatius of Antioch.

12. Rejection of heresies by reference to the teaching handed down in cities founded by Apostles—i.e. tradition itself, and the connection of Tradition with Episcopacy as in Irenaeus and Tertullian.

13. Redemption as atonement, or "satisfaction."

14. Use of *eikons* and images in churches.

15. In general, against heretics, although appeal was made to Scripture, nevertheless the first and final argument was that

the heretic taught something different. This is clear from the history of

Sabellius—cf. Denis of Alexandria.
Arius—cf. Athanasius.
Nestorius—cf. Cyril of Alexandria.
Eutyches—cf. Leo the Great.

Here I should also put the rejection of the Macedonians, by people like St. Basil the Great; and even today, if one wants to show from Scripture alone that the Holy Spirit is a distinct person—hypostasis, persona—the argument against people like Cyril Richardson is not easy; but the "mind" of the Church, or Tradition, is sufficient.

16. In general the norm: *quod semper, quod ubique, quod ab omnibus. . . .*

But, "Tradition" cannot be understood apart from the promise of the Holy Spirit, who shall lead us into all truth. . . .

Here, too, arises the difficult question of the "development" of doctrine. Newman tried to face the question: by what norm can we distinguish authentic developments from corruptions? His answer, to speak roughly, was that this norm is the coherency of the particular development with the whole "mind" of the Church.

The Report on *Ways of Worship* presented by the Indian section contained discussions of accommodation of Christian institutions and calendar to indigenous national feasts and images. A Catholic priest wrote an account of liturgical developments in the Catholic Church. It is in the field of liturgy that development among Protestants has been most noticeable: in newly built churches, the altar—in many cases—supplants the pulpit or the table, and at Lund there seemed general agreement that the Eucharist is the normal Christian worship, other services being either a preparation for, or a thanksgiving after, the Eucharist.

In the Report on Ways of Worship, one may be surprised at the omission to treat two questions: the nature of the Eucharist and the nature of episcopacy and its connection with apostolic succession and with a "valid" ministry. I think that the reason for this omission is that particular churches are in process of discussing these questions and that the Faith and Order Commission judges it best not to intervene at present, but to await the outcome of some of these more local discussions.

For ten years, 1947-57, conversations had proceeded between theologians of the Lutheran, Reformed and United traditions, and the result was published in 1957 in the form of "theses," known as "the Arnoldshain Theses on Holy Communion," which indicated very considerable agreement, though the publication occasioned theological debate, which is still continuing.[8] The theses seem to me very disappointing. However they are not regarded as final and discussion is still continuing.

Episcopacy, in several proposed church unions, has been proposed for practical acceptance in such sort that all ministers will be episcopally ordained but without exact interpretation of the nature of "the historic episcopate" or of episcopal ordination. A Catholic may perhaps judge that there is here a compromise of doctrine, or an admission of the possibility of people holding contradictory doctrines about a fundamental of the faith. Before so concluding, however, a Catholic ought to take into account the views of some Anglo-Catholics about apostolic succession and about the function of episcopacy. A. J. Mason, Gregory Dix and Lionel Thornton, whom many follow, held that Confirmation by a bishop is necessary in order to make a member of the Church, so that without Confirmation no one can be admitted to Holy Communion, and ordination of a non-confirmed man would be invalid. Anglo-Catholics, too, sometimes presented the need of "tactual succession" in a far more mechanical way than do Catholics. The permission of ordination without interpretation of the nature of episcopacy may well envisage these Anglo-Catholic views, acceptance of which is not in fact required in Catholic ordinations. Moreover, about the "validity" of Orders there is immense misunderstanding, and to many non-episcopalians to accept episcopacy as a means of securing "valid" orders implies an admission that their ministry hitherto has been "a spurious imitation" without the blessing of God on it. Much more could be said on this topic.[9]

---

[8]Cf. "The Conversations concerning Holy Communion in the German Evangelical Church," *Ecumenical Review* 9:2 (January, 1959), pp. 188-91 and 201.

[9]See the 2nd edition of *Principles of Sacramental Theology,* 1960, pp. 650-53.

Judgment about "reunions." In judging all these "mergers" we Catholics should use two standards: first, our own doctrinal position; and second, the previous doctrinal position of the units prior to the merger.

The fundamental question to ask is: is the merger better or worse than the previous position? Does it tend away from Catholic truth and life, or does it on the whole tend towards Catholicity? Does it tend to increase loyalty to the heretical Reformers, or does it tend to loyalty to the one Church of Christ? In many cases the dropping of the old name, indicative of a denomination—v.g. Lutheran, Wesleyan, Methodist, Reformed, Presbyterian, Protestant, Disciples, Anglican, Congregationalist, Baptist—tends to widen the spiritual horizon and carry thoughts and ideals towards unity with the whole Church throughout all history as against unity merely with the denomination since its comparatively recent beginning. In the negotiations, for example, between the Anglicans and the Presbyterians, the latter called frank attention to the erastianism of the Church of England, saying clearly that a Church ought to be free from the State in matters of liturgy and in nomination of its bishops and dignitaries. Partly for this reason, it may be conjectured, Archbishop Ramsey has said that he will work for greater liberty for the Church of England. All this, however, is a digression. To return to *Ways of Worship*, the Indian report put the whole matter of liturgy and of Christian worship in a setting far wider than that to which European and American Protestants have been accustomed, and to a considerable extent forces them to face the problems of the universality of the Christian appeal, and so to be ready to modify customs which grew up since the sixteenth century, to study Eastern liturgies and to restore the sense of mystery and of awe in Christian worship.

The studies on *Institutionalism* have been to a considerable extent directed by "the sociological approach." The attempt is at an accumulation of ordered knowledge about the churches as human societies, with their methods of organization and administration; to some extent it may be regarded as a study of what canon law exists among diverse Christian bodies. On the fringe of these studies lies a book like Paul Harrison's *Authority and Power in the Free Church Tradition. A Social Case Study of the American Baptist Convention* (Princeton University Press, 1959). In the background, of course, lies the question of the authority of the church and of its distribution among different subsidiary persons or groups.

4. *A continuing atonement.* These theological Commissions of the Faith and Order are only one element, though an important element, in the whole ecumenical movement. Here I note one idea which recurs in a good deal of writing by ecumenists, that the Atonement of Christ is continued in the Church. This is a reversal of the old Protestant conviction that Christ's work was done finally and fully on the cross and that each individual had only to have trust that Christ had won forgiveness for him. Now it is far more generally appreciated that Christ's work, though fully accomplished on the cross, is still timelessly prolonged in the Church, which in mysterious but true fashion is identified with "the suffering servant" of Isaiah, and with Christ works for the salvation of all men.

5. *A growing consciousness* of the Catholic Church has been shown by a number of works which attempt serious study of the Church. Walther von Lowenich, in his *Modern Roman Catholicism,* is most certainly unfriendly and his book is really an attack. Nevertheless he admits that the Catholic Church has preserved "a supernatural dimension," and has held its faithful far better than have the Protestant Churches. Professor Jaroslav Pelikan's *The Riddle of Roman Catholicism* is in many ways incoherent and very illogical, and yet he makes a serious effort to understand. K.E. Skydsgaard's *Protestantism and Catholicism* simply confronts the two outlooks and does not do much to reconcile them; yet Skydsgaard also makes a definite effort to understand; his study of Catholicism is being continued and his outlook is definitely being broadened. At St. Andrews in 1960 he accepted very graciously and humbly some Catholic reflections on his paper on Tradition. Cullmann, of Switzerland, is so impressed with the need of Catholic-Protestant rapprochement that he suggested taking up collections of money in Protestant Churches to be given to Catholic poor parishes, and collections

to be taken in Catholic Churches to be given to Protestant poor. The concrete suggestion has had, apparently, some success in Switzerland, though I doubt if it is practical in most parts of the world. Nevertheless, Cullmann (whose book on St. Peter marks a definite advance), asserts a principle of great importance: *reconciliation can only come by sacrifice.*

Dr. Robert McAfee Brown, of the Union Theological Seminary, in *An American Dialogue,* does a good deal to dissolve Protestant prejudice and writes in a spirit of sincere charity. At the end, of course, he declares that two matters are unacceptable to Protestants, the infallibility of the Pope and the definition of the Assumption. But Brown, sensing the irreconcilability, refuses to acquiesce: no Christian, he says, has a right to judge by what is merely humanly possible: it is God with whom the ultimate rests and what is impossible to men is possible to God. Brown, moreover, says that his own contribution only prepares the ground for dialogue; and on this he speaks wisely. The "war-psychology" must be destroyed and men must look solely for truth and not for the victory of a competing social group.

The recently translated book by Leon Christiani and Jean Rilliet, *Catholics and Protestants, Separated Brothers,* (Newman Press, 1961) though the dialogue does not advance very far, is another indication of "openness" to Catholic ideas.[10]

The September 1960 issue of *The Lutheran World* contains two statements indicative of readiness to listen and learn. In an article entitled "On Dialogue between Roman Catholic and Evangelical Lutheran Theologians," Dr. K.E. Skydsgaard says:

"To be honest, means also that we dare to make this self-confession: Here in humility and joy I have learned something new which I did not know before. I simply must correct my former opinion because during this conversation a new and

---

[10]In Germany the following are noteworthy: *Begegnung der Christen: Studien Evangelischer und Katholischer Theologen.* Herauggegeben von Maximilian Roesle und Oscar Cullmann. Frankfort am Main. 1960: *Gespräch zwischen den Konfessionen.* Von Hans Asmussen und Thomas Sartory. Frankfurt am Main. 1959: *Die Katholizität der Kirche. Beitrage zum Gespräch zwischen der Evangelischen und der Römisch-Katholischen Kirche.* Von Hans Asmussen und Wilhelm Stählin. Stuttgart. 1957.

surprising insight was granted me. Whoever closes his mind to such possibilities is not mature enough for interconfessional conversations. Why should a Lutheran be ashamed to admit that in many respects the Roman Catholic Church has preserved a primitive Christian tradition which we have lost? The opposite should also not be impossible!" (*art. cit.*, p. 137).

He ends by saying:

"Despite all of our deepest differences, we have a great responsibility towards one another. We cannot live without each other, because Christ is the Lord of his Christian people" (p. 141).

In the same issue, Professor George A. Lindbeck, of Yale, wrote on "The Evangelical Possibilities of Roman Catholic Theology." He urges that "we (Lutherans) should always begin by asking what is the best theological interpretation which can be put on such and such a dogma," and after illustrating this by reference to books like Congar's *Vraie et Fausse Réforme dans l'Eglise* (1950), Bouyer's *Du protestantisme à l'Eglise,* and Küng's *Rechtfertigung: Die Lehre Karl Barths und eine katholische Besinnung* (1957) ends with the following words about the papacy:

"In concluding this article, it should be emphasized that we have examined only a few of the evangelical possibilities of Roman Catholic thought. We have not discussed sacramental theology, nor mystical and monastic piety, nor those most painful of all problems which centre round Mary, the church and the papacy. However, we should never forget that, even in these last-named areas, there are more, as well as less, evangelical ways of adhering to the Roman position. There is, for example, all the difference in the world between integralists who consider papal pronouncements as the fount of all Christian wisdom, and those who regard the pope as a fallible human being, perhaps wicked, conceivably even damned, whom God, in his infinite mercy, prevents from positively misleading the Church on at least those rare occasions when he proclaims dogma. Men who think in this latter way are clearly trying to be faithful, even in their theology, to the same Lord whom we wish to serve, and so we must approach their thought with genuine openness, a lack of Confessional defensiveness, and a deep desire to hear the truth spoken without any regard to whether it is labelled 'Lutheran' or 'Roman'" (*art. cit.*, p. 151-2).

A Catholic, of course, may well lift his eyebrows a bit at the way Professor Lindbeck phrases things. At the same time, even on topics which he regards as "painful," Dr. Lindbeck is willing to listen and to open his mind to the truth.

3. *Catholic Influence*

My last topic concerns the extent to which non-Catholics can be influenced by Catholics, and, more particularly by theologians.

Here, I venture to give an opinion of my own:

The first and essential service a Catholic theologian can contribute to the ecumenical cause is to know Catholic theology and to advance serenely in understanding the faith without paying too much attention to what is specifically non-Catholic. I put this carefully: "to what is specifically non-Catholic." Men who in fact are non-Catholics may be admirable scholars and may have individual insights which are thoroughly correct. One example of this is non-Catholic biblical scholarship, to which Catholic scholars have been and continue to be heavily indebted. I instance C.H. Dodd, C.K. Barrett, W.F. Albright, Vincent Taylor. It is needless to mention dictionaries, concordances, archaeology, semantics and the whole sweep of ancient history and literature. Another example is patristic study, on which non-Catholics have contributed so very much, for instance, editing better texts of the Fathers, identifying and dating authentic works, translating, and in general making invaluable historical, linguistic and even theological contributions. Merely in passing I mention the work of F.W. Cross on St. Athanasius, and of J.N.D. Kelly on the creeds, and of the Australian, John McIntyre, on St. Anselm. The list could be extended.

These men write with the most admirable erudition in the most limpid English, and we can and do profit from their writings and from many of their insights and useful hypotheses. Nevertheless I believe that Catholic theology in the main should proceed calmly on its own way and develop along its own lines, with only incidental attention to apologetics. The best apologetic will be the power and force of the truth of the authentic Christian tradition presented uncontroversially and non-apologetically, presented with disinterested objectivity.

This has two corollaries:

a. Catholic *theological students* during their philosophical and theological courses need not pay more than incidental attention to contemporary controversies or to the "ecumenical dialogue."

b. Catholic *post-graduate* and *research students* need not feel too great an impulse to select topics which seem of immediate interest in "the ecumenical dialogue."

Theological training. As to the first of these, the general theological course given in our Universities and Seminaries, I am well aware that voices have been raised against an undue "scholastic" or even "rationalistic" approach to the detriment of the scriptural, patristic, liturgical and historical. Complaints have been heard against "the manuals" and "the text-book" method and against what is called "Denzinger theology"; the training has been said to induce reliance on mere formulae, generally latinized, on an excessive systematization and on an "essentialist" abstraction blind to the existential situation of humanity. Now, any method of studying theology is open to objections and is open to misuse, and I have in my time criticized many text-books. Yet some critics seem to me to miss the real strength of our method. No man can know everything in scripture, patristics, liturgy and history; some method of selection is essential, and the method accepted in Catholic theological schools is to cover the whole field in outline and main principles and to leave details to be filled in later. It is like a doctor studying anatomy: he must know the general structure and something of the articulation. A Catholic theological student in his ordinary course, is given the anatomy and something of the articulation of all the parts of the Christian tradition and outlook. In all his subsequent reading and discussion he has fixed points of reference and of judgment: he knows—or should know—what is part of the faith and what is disputable; he may perhaps be superficial but he is usually clear; above all, he has an instinct—if his training has been sound—for the true faith as against distortions, excessive simplifications and undue reliance on outlooks which reflect the fashion of time. What is "modern" in 1920 is old-fashioned in 1960; and what is accepted as "contemporary" in 1960 is out of date by 1980. In this a difference clearly appears between Catholic theology and non-Catholic. The "quest of the historical Jesus" once held practically the whole interest of non-Catholic studies; then "eschatology" came in and everything had to be "eschatological." Now eschatology is fading out and "demythologizing" is in fashion on the one side and a revitalized "evangelicalism" or even a new form of "fundamentalism" on the other. Men like Carl Henry, and John Packer, and the "neo-evangelicals," will have no truck with the "crisis-theology" of Brunner and Barth. Undoubtedly these fashions and disagreements open minds, stimulate investigation and contribute to theological knowledge; at the same time much energy may be expended fruitlessly and even deleteriously. The firm outline of Catholic theology, which reached a basic synthesis in the middle ages, by summarizing the patristic and scriptural tradition, may by some have been regarded as unduly conservative or even narrow; yet it was one main factor in saving the faith of the millions and in laying the necessary foundations for what may be called revitalized theology and the advances of which we see so much evidence today. A simple message, delivered with conviction and authority, can hold the hearts of men and can arouse their faith and their generosity. Our theological schools (to omit for the moment the all-important work of God's grace and of personal holiness) in the main have succeeded in turning out priests who could and did present a simple message with conviction and with authority, and this, surely, is an evangelical ideal. No doubt, things can and will be improved; but in my judgment it must be an improvement in the use of the method and not any radical change of method. St. Thomas and St. Bonaventure are still contemporary.

Two indications occur to illustrate the excellence of the general system of Catholic theological training. The first, that Dr. R.A. Brown, on the question of presenting doctrine correctly, remarked that there would be small difficulty on the Catholic side, as Catholic theologians usually knew their stuff. I hope he was not too optimistic, but his remark is a tribute to our training.

The second indication is contained in two Surveys of the Training of the Ministry in Madagascar and in Africa, the first, by Dr. C.W. Ranson, Dr. F. Birkeli, Professor F. Michaeli and Rev. T. Rasendrahasina,[11] the second by Dr. Norman Goodall and Rev. Eric W. Nielsen.[12] Both of these surveys insist on the need to strengthen the teaching of what we call dogmatic theology and they systematic theology. The Madagascar Report says this:

"Systematic Theology (or Christian Dogmatics) is in our view one of the subjects on which thorough, sound teaching ought to be given. Yet the teaching actually given in the present theological schools is sometimes very restricted, if not completely lacking. We are not thinking of the kind of doctrinal teaching which might be called "denominational," which would vary from one church to another. We would refer to the doctrine common to every Christian Church, because it is Biblical doctrine. A precise, systematic knowledge of *Christian doctrine,* the foundations of which are given by the Bible, is absolutely indispensable if the pastor is to instruct his flock in the teaching the enemies of the Gospel faith."

Much the same was indicated in the African Report.

The practical point of these remarks about our theological

---

[11]Dr. Charles W. Ranson, General Secretary of the International Missionary Council (London and New York), chairman of the Commission. Dr. Fridtjov Birkeli, director of the Department of World Missions in the Lutheran World Federation (Geneva). Professor Frank Michaeli, professor of Old Testament studies at the Free Faculty of Protestant Theology (Paris). Rev. T. Rasendrahasina, General Secretary of the Imerina Synod of the London Missionary Society (Tananarive).

It will be noticed that the members of this Commission represented differing national and ecclesiastical traditions, and they also brought to their task personal experience of missionary work.

[12]Dr. Norman Goodall has been Secretary in London of the Joint Committee of the World Council of Churches and International Missionary Council. Dr. Eric Nielsen is Secretary of the International Missionary Council Study Department.

courses is to deprecate early specialization. There is, of course, no doubt that a student's interest in a particular aspect or problem of theology can be a great help, and can be something of a searchlight to illumine other parts of theology. But a searchlight has a special function. It concentrates a powerful beam on a strictly limited field, but it leaves the surrounding area in darkness. Just so specialization tends to take things out of their setting. The ordinary course of theology throws a weaker and a more diffused light; but, while details may be left in shadow, the whole field of theology is illuminated and truths can be seen in their relation to one another. The illustration limps, of course. But it would be, for instance, of small ultimate use for a student to specialize on the theology of the laity before he has a firm grasp on the theology of original sin, or on the Eucharist and liturgy, without a good understanding of the doctrine of the atonement, or on the nature of the unity of the Church without a knowledge of the unity of Godhead and manhood in one Christ. Mistakes about the hypostatic union will inevitably reflect themselves in mistakes about the unity of the Church, and *vice versa.*

Two matters, however, are of greater importance in our day than ever before: theological terminology, and the interpretation of expressions of the Church's teaching. As to terminology, our separated brethren are generally quite ignorant of Aristotelian categories and of the words used, for instance, by St. Thomas and St. Bonaventure. They easily misunderstand words like *substance, substantial form, accident, nature, essence, formal cause, first cause, matter, material cause, infused habit, moral, virtue, spiritual,* and even *person* and *personality.* Here, I confess, is a problem to which I can see no easy theoretical solution. Theology is a science and it is impossible for any science not to have its own technical language, and to some extent the terminology is embedded in the content of the Christian message itself. There is no solution, I am convinced, in the suggestion of a return to language exclusively biblical; for the problem returns since Bultmann and others declare that biblical language is a foreign language to modern technical (or organizational) man. The fact is that a people or a nation cannot be understood without knowing the language of the country; and a religion cannot be understood without knowing its peculiar language. A certain amount of scholastic language has become part of the Catholic religion, and to a considerable extent—if one compares East and West—part of the Western cultural inheritance. To surrender it would involve more than a surrender of language, for language is closely connected with thought. And yet, I think an effort should be made to make clear the meaning of our traditional language and to avoid technical terms which can mislead or mystify. [Note: Here I merely mention the underlying problems of the relation of philosophy to theology.] The English sometimes used in theological writings is nothing less than barbarous and well calculated to repel uninitiated though cultured readers. Theology is developing and its language is developing also.

The *interpretation of authoritative pronouncements* such as definitions by Councils is a matter of greater importance today than ever before. Here I confess to an antipathy to "Denzinger theology": too often it cites a canon with strong emphasis on the "anathema sit," without sufficient regard to the historical background of the Canon and its real intent, and without sufficient examination of the meaning of "anathema sit." Too often authorities are cited as if they settled the matter; for Catholics, of course, they do settle the matter (though even they like to understand why the authority is justified), but for non-Catholics mere authority—even scriptural authority unless carefully presented—does not settle the matter. An experience of nine years of lectures at the Newman Institute in London—to an audience intelligent on the whole but theologically unformed—convinced me that for the average layman or woman it is reason rather than authority which satisfies. Sometimes what we call *rationes convenientiae* carry more practical weight than any number of *auctoritates*.

General theological influence. So much about our ordinary theological training. As regards the influence which Catholic theologians can have, my feeling is that in the long run this will be indirect rather than direct, or, to put it another way, long-term rather than short-term. At the moment, two matters are obvious, first, a change of spirit, which is an essential—a change from being antagonists and adversaries to being truly brethren even though separated; and second, what is called "dialogue," that is confrontation of different doctrines and attitudes, an admirable example of which is the book written by Fr. Weigel and Dr. McAfee Brown called *An American Dialogue*. This method may be a necessary first step and has initial advantages, principally in dissipating false ideas about the doctrine and the life of others. It can introduce those who participate into a world they did not know existed and can greatly increase mutual respect and good feeling. It can reveal that not seldom people are trying to say the same things though in different language. But this method of "dialogue" has definite limits: though some misunderstandings may be cleared up, mere understanding of a doctrine may only increase and sharpen disagreement with it. Moreover, it is, so to speak, a self-conscious approach: our relationships to one another: what *you* hold, what *we* hold. The danger is that each party may try to prove he is right and the other wrong. There is another method. People are more drawn together by a common interest in something outside themselves than by discussion of their own relationships; this is true theologically as well as personally.

Missions. The number of Christians in the world is steadily, though relatively, decreasing. Unhappily, divisions between Christians confuse, perplex and repel non-Christians, who ask: "To what are we being invited to convert ourselves? You exhort us to abandon our traditional religion—for what? For Anglicanism, Congregationalism, Methodism, Presbyterianism, Adventism, Mormonism—or what? We want to be Christians and nothing else; but your divisions simply confuse us."

This is a most potent motive for working for the consolidation of Christian effort, for avoiding, as far as can rightly be, competition, and for zeal for the unity of all Christians. This motive, however, quite apart, there is a certain common ground among Christians in defining exactly the ultimate reason for missions, in discovering the best methods to use among different peoples and the problems to be faced. Missiologists, Catholic and Protestant, can and do learn from one another much about non-Christian religions and the best methods of approach to them; for instance, the books of Sweetman and of Kenneth Cragg on the Christian approach to Islam can be of general help, and the bibliographical material published in the *International Review of Missions* is most useful, as is the statistical matter gathered by the Missionary Research Library in New York.

I am far from suggesting that Catholics should approve, much less help, Protestant missions—the more especially as 75 per cent of the "missionaries" who go from North America to Latin America stand entirely aloof from the World Council and the International Missionary Council and are generally hostile to Catholicism. But I do suggest that the whole question of unity should be viewed in the perspective of the mission of the Church to convert the whole world, and that much information can be gained from the missionary activity of Protestants. The Report on "Proselytism," for instance, published in the *Ecumenical Review*, October, 1960, could be quoted with profit when some Protestants are aggressive and objectionable.

Christology. Bishop John Wright of Pittsburgh, in a symposium on "dialogue" in *America*, Jan. 14, 1961, hit a very important nail on the head: it is on meditation upon Christ, and upon the Incarnation that main hope is to be placed. Protestant theologians are only beginning to awake to Christology. They do, indeed, more and more accept Nicaea and Chalcedon. Nevertheless, there is a whole world of Catholic theology in Christology which is utterly unknown to them. Modern non-Catholic writers on Christology,[13] though they manifest the recent trend towards an orthodox Christology and though they have much very useful matter on Scripture, nevertheless show that it is impossible to read the New Testament without some antecedent assumption, and that the antecedent conditions the findings. These writers either omit or confuse questions such as Christ's human awareness of his Godhead and of all involved in his redemptive work. Here is a fruitful source of common under-

---

[13]Donal Baillie, *God Was in Christ*, five reprintings, new edition 1955; Vincent Taylor, *The Person of Christ in New Testament Teaching*, London, 1958; Oscar Cullmann, *The Christology of the New Testament*, English translation 1959; W. Norman Pittenger, *The Word Incarnate, A Study of the Doctrine of the Person of Christ;* Maurice Relton, *Studies in Christology*, London, 1960. These writers are characteristic of different schools and their books are highly esteemed.

standing: What is involved in St. Paul's "he loved me and delivered himself up for me" (Gal. 2:20)? Was it a human love, or was it only a divine love? The answer to this question involves far more than is at first apparent.

Christology and missiology are merely examples. In the long run the best ecumenical service will lie in an increased vitality of Catholic theology in all its varieties, scriptural, patristic, liturgical, historical, ascetical as well as ecclesiological.

It is the truth of God which must enlighten minds and bring unity in thought and conviction; and the truth of God is all-pervading. Many minds and many different forms of presentation are needed, though grace and charity in presentation are always essential. Controversy has its place, though in our time, a very restricted place, since controversy tends to lessen charity and charity is needed to say the truth. "We must love one another," said Archbishop Heenan, "until we come to see the same truth."

Lastly theology needs men, time and money. Scholarly work takes time; it needs books which are expensive, and it can often be helped by travel and personal contact with other scholars. Moreover, it seldom produces immediate tangible results, but its influence is slow and cumulative. In this, as in life, it is needful to lose one's life to find it. Far, far too many capable men are taken from scholarly work and assigned to administration. Yet plans must be laid, not for the next five years, nor the next ten, but for the next fifty. And there again may be verified our Savior's words: "I have sent you to reap that on which you did not labour: others have laboured and you have entered into their labours."

Prayer and Christian Unity

by Angelus Delahunt, S.A.

The cause of unity to which the Society of the Atonement is totally dedicated and for which so many others both within the Catholic Church and outside of it labor so tirelessly had its inspiration in the upper room where Christ had gathered with his twelve on the night before he died. After having given us the sacrament of his love, the Holy Eucharist, which is the sacrament of unity as well, Jesus prayed to his heavenly Father, first for his very own, and then for all those who would come to believe in him through their ministry.

"Yet not for these only do I pray," he implored his Father in heaven, "but for those also who through their word are to believe in me, that all may be one, even as thou, Father, in me and I in thee; that they also may be one in us, that the world may believe that thou hast sent me" (John 17:20-21).

This prayer for the unity of his followers became the inspiration for the tremendous apostolate in behalf of Christian unity instituted by our saintly founder, the late Father Paul James Francis, when he originated the Chair of Unity Octave more than half a century ago while still an Episcopalian clergyman. Today under the influence of God's grace this eight-day period of prayer for Christian unity is world-wide in scope as well as in observance.

Like the grain of mustard seed described by our blessed Lord in one of his parables as "the smallest of all the seeds" (Matt. 13:32), the seed planted here on the Mount of the Atonement in 1908 has taken root deeply and has developed into a great and noble tree that can be seen far and wide "so that the birds of the air come and dwell in its branches."

Prior to the establishment of the Chair of Unity Octave there was little or no concern among the Catholic faithful with the perplexing and agonizing problem of a divided Christendom. Schism and heresy did not seem to disturb the rank and file of those who professed to be members of the Mystical Body of Christ.

In the providence of God it was given to Father Paul to play the decisive role in alerting Catholic people to the deep and constant longing of their holy Mother the Church to bring back to the fold of Christ those of her children who had erred and strayed far from her. Though primarily a prayer movement, the Chair of Unity Octave has served yet another useful purpose. It has taken this vastly complex and complicated problem of Christian unity from the realm of the purely theological to the level of popular consumption. There is no doubt but that as a result of this annual period of prayer millions of people are not only praying for Christian unity but understand a little better the urgency of this cause and their personal responsibility toward its ultimate solution.

It is remarkable that once the interest had been stimulated in the cause of unity there was no lack of either enthusiasm or response. From the very beginning the appeals of Father Paul to Catholics and Protestants alike all over the world to join with him and his community in praying "*ut omnes unum sint*" were very favorably received.

Then as now, the power of humble and fervent prayer for the fulfillment of Christ's prayer for unity was emphasized. The Catholic faithful especially were made to realize that this was an apostolate of immediate concern to them, that this was not the sole responsibility of the hierarchy and the clergy.

And since the sublime objective of the Chair of Unity Octave is one so obviously in accord with the manifest will of Christ, its ultimate realization is assured, contingent only upon our perseverance in prayer and penance and God's design for its actual solution. For did not Christ himself declare: "And other sheep I have that are not of this fold. Them also I must bring, and they shall hear my voice, and *there shall be one fold and one shepherd*" (John 10:16).

God has blessed abundantly this universal chorus of prayer that has ascended to heaven without interruption ever since the first Chair of Unity Octave was observed in 1908. Among the first visible fruits of this prayer was the conversion of its originator, Father Paul James Francis, and his community of Friars and Sisters which took place in 1909.

At about the same time a group of Episcopalian clergymen under the dynamic leadership of the renowned William McGarvey of Philadelphia also came into the Catholic Church. A few years later the Benedictine monks of Caldy in England made corporate submission to the Holy See and continue today as a religious community.

More recently the mass conversion of a noteworthy segment of the ancient but dissident Malabar Church in South India caused a not inconsiderable stir within ecumenical circles. It is gratifying to note that their spiritual leader, the late Archbishop Mar Ivanios, in a letter to our founder, attributed the reconciliation of his flock with the See of Peter directly to the influence of the Chair of Unity Octave.

There are other important results that have stemmed from this prayer movement. Inspired by the unselfish motives that have impelled Catholics to work and pray so diligently for the reunion of Christendom, countless numbers of Protestants of good will have joined in this veritable crusade of prayer. Each year throughout the length and breadth of this globe they join their prayers to ours "that all may be one."

One of the truly exciting spiritual phenomena of our times is that today Protestants are themselves acutely aware of the distressing nature of this problem and are themselves sincerely and humbly seeking ways and means to remedy what they describe as "the scandal of divisions." This is a development that should encourage all who labor for the cause of unity.

The Chair of Unity Octave, therefore, has played a not inconsequential role in molding the minds and hearts of men of good will everywhere to see the problem for what it really is and to seek avenues that will lead to its ultimate solution. This octave of prayer has been the God-inspired instrument by which Christians have been advised of and awakened to the urgent need for unity among themselves not only because it is the manifest will of Christ but also because only a united Christian world can effectively counteract the common threat today posed by militant atheistic Communism.

So if for no other reasons, Christians everywhere owe an immeasurable debt of gratitude to the vision and initiative of the humble man of God who originated this great movement for Christian Unity. For me to say anything more in tribute to Father Paul for inaugurating this worldwide movement of prayer which has succeeded in directing the gaze of all mankind towards Rome and the Chair of St. Peter would be superfluous. You who have worked long and tirelessly in the field of ecumenism already recognize the impact of this man's ideal of "one fold and one shepherd."

Suffice it for me to state that the reasons which prompted the establishment of the Chair of Unity Octave in 1908 are all the more urgent today. Today the religious world presents a profile radically different from that of fifty years ago. More than ever before peoples of every nation and of every religious persuasion are interested in ecumenism and with every fibre of their being desire to see a world of one faith. Hence it is no exaggeration to say that it is far more imperative to muster the spiritual forces of the Chair of Unity Octave today than it was in 1908. We are perhaps on the threshold of a "breakthrough," as they say in scientific circles.

With humility and perseverance we must continue to do, and even extend this great prayer movement, this apostolate initiated by Father Paul. It is at once a privilege and a responsibility to join our prayers with the priestly prayer of Christ for the at-one-ment of our separated brethren through reconciliation with His Church.

We are all aware that the cause of unity among those of our brethren not guided by the magisterium of the Church, and left a prey to the aberrations of human error and frailty, is seriously threatened. The goal, because humanly unattainable, could easily begin to appear utopian to them. They could satisfy themselves with a solution of compromise and relegate the universal profession of a single faith to the perfections of the world to come.

The Cardinal Archbishop of Utrecht sounded a warning

along this line when he recently addressed a gathering of Catholics and Protestants in the Netherlands. He said in part: "Truly the danger is not imaginary that we feel content with a seeming unity, not troubling ourselves any longer about the pure and undivided unity which the Lord meant when speaking of himself being one with the Father."

The prayers which millions of souls each year offer in behalf of Christian Unity as a result of the Chair of Unity Octave will indeed play a decisive role in bringing about the yearned for goal of "one fold and one shepherd." There can be no doubt about this. It is true that there are other ways and other means that should be and must be utilized in the cause of ecumenism. But in the final analysis it is prayer, at once humble, fervent and persevering, that will obtain the grace, or graces, necessary "that all may be one."

It is most gratifying, therefore, to note that both the late beloved Pope Pius XII and our present Holy Father, Pope John XXIII, have emphasized the importance of prayer for bringing about Christian unity.

In an autograph letter addressed to His Eminence, Francis Cardinal Spellman, Archbishop of New York, on the occasion of the Golden Jubilee of the Chair of Unity Octave, Pope Pius XII said: "And so even though there may be numerous works of the apostolate to bring this plan into effect, nevertheless we believe that there is no better manner of accomplishing it than by offering humble and earnest prayer to God. . . . We desire, therefore, that this Octave of Prayer be spread everywhere in the world as far as possible."

More recently in commemoration of the fiftieth anniversary of the reception of the Society of the Atonement into the Fold of Peter, His Holiness, Pope John XXIII, in an autograph letter to us, declared:

"Prayer, in fact, is the first and principal means to be used to bring about this yearned-for unity, as your beloved founder, Father Paul Wattson, so clearly saw; and he therefore promoted the Chair of Unity Octave, during which fervent supplications should be raised to the Almighty for the return of all to the one true Faith.

"We gladly make Our own the words of Our immediate

predecessor of happy memory, Pope Pius XII, by expressing the prayerful wish that this practice 'be spread everywhere in the world as widely as possible,' especially in view of the forthcoming General Council, during which it is hoped that our separated brethren will be copiously illuminated and strengthened by the Divine Comforter."

With these warm and cordial words of commendation ringing in our ears, let us one and all rededicate our prayers and labors in the cause of unity with renewed fervor, renewed humility, renewed perseverance. Let us in the spirit of that upper room where the first Christians awaited the coming of the Paraclete by remaining steadfast in prayer with Mary, the Mother of Jesus, turn with the same confidence to her. May she whom we lovingly invoke under the glorious title of Our Lady of the Atonement guide us in our work and intercede in our behalf with her Divine Son that soon but in God's own good time "all may be one."

Appendix

LIST OF PAPERS AND ARTICLES
prepared for the Commission during 1960
(Fourth supplement to the list of November 1956)

This list records all papers prepared for the Faith and Order Commission and the Theological Commissions during 1960. Copies of papers marked* are still available, and can be sent to anyone who would be interested to receive them. Prices of printed papers are indicated; a charge of Sw.Fr.0.50 is made for mimeographed papers.

m–mimeographed

Faith and Order Numbered Papers

*FOC Paper no. 28: Survey of Church Union Negotiations 1957-59. (Offprint from *The Ecumenical Review* Vol. XII No. 2, January 1960.) Sw.Fr.1.–; 1s.8d.; $0.25.

FOC Paper no. 29: *One Lord, One Baptism.* Report on "The Divine Trinity and the Unity of the Church" and Report on "The Meaning of Baptism."
SCM Press: (Studies in Ministry and Worship, 17), London, 1960. 6s (Obtainable from bookshops and SCM Press; not available from WCC, Geneva).
American Edition: Published by Augsburg Publishing House, Minneapolis, USA, 1961.

*FOC Paper no. 30: *Orthodoxy; a Faith and Order Dialogue.* (Reprinted from *The Ecumenical Review* Vol. XII no. 2, January 1960.) Sw.Fr.3.–; 4s.; $1.–.

*FOC Paper no. 31: Minutes of the Faith and Order Commission meeting, St. Andrews, 3-8 August 1960. Sw.Fr.4.50; 7s6d.; $1.50.

Theological Commission on Christ and the Church

**The Meaning of Baptism for the Unity of the Church: The Evolution of an Ecumenical Statement.* (Offprint from *Encounter* no. 21:3, Summer 1960.) (This pamphlet gathers together the various papers and memoranda on baptism produced by the Faith & Order Commission and the TCCC between 1957 and 1960.) Sw.Fr.2.–; 3s.4d.; $0.50.

**Comments on "The Meaning of Baptism"* received from various sources during 1960. m.

G.R. Cragg: Schemes of Church Union and the Concerns of the Faith and Order Commission. (Prepared for the meeting of the North American Section at New Haven, June 1960.) m.

*M.A. Creasey: Notes on books on the Holy Spirit by J.E. Fison, H.P. Van Dusen and F.W. Dillistone. 1960. m.

*F.V. Filson: Summary of A.B. Come's *Human Spirit and Holy Spirit.* 1960. m.

F.V. Filson: The Holy Spirit in the New Testament. (Prepared for the meeting of the North American Section at New Haven, June 1960.) m.

*E.R. Hardy: Summary of R. Prenter's *Spiritus Creator.* 1960 m.

W. Harrelson: *Israel and the Spirit.* (Prepared for the meeting of the North American Section at New Haven, June 1960.) m.

*T.A. Kantonen: Summary of articles in RGG on "Geist." 1960. m.

*J.R. Nelson: Summary of Théo Preiss's "Le Témoignage intérieur du Saint-Esprit." 1960. m.

*A. Nygren: Zusammenfassung von J.L. Leuba: *Institution und Ereignis.* 1960. m.

Theological Commission on Worship

*Draft Interim Report, 1960. Prepared by the European Section at its meeting at Taizé, April 1960. m.

**Worship and the Church's Mission and Unity.* A report of the Third Indian Conference on Worship, held at Bangalore, May 26-30, 1960. Rs.1.50; Sw.Fr. 1.50; 2s.6d. $0.50.

*Report of Meeting on Worship, Tokyo, Japan, January 1960. m.

*Worship Trends in the Philippines: a report. 1960. m.

W. Hahn: Die verschiedenartige Struktur liturgischer Aussagen in den grossen Kirchen und theologischen Traditionen. (Prepared for the meeting of the European Section at Taizé, April 1960.) m.
English translation: The different forms of liturgical expression in the great churches and theological traditions.

*J.C. Rylaarsdam: The Matrix of Worship in the Old Testament. (Prepared for the American Section). 1960. m.

*M.H. Shepherd: The Origin of the Church's Liturgy. (Prepared for the American Section.) 1960. m.

C. Westermann: Der Sonntag als Tag des Herrn. (Prepared

for the meeting of the European Section at Taizé, April 1960.) m.
English translation: Sunday as the Lord's Day. m.

Theological Commission on Tradition & Traditions

*Bibliography on the Problem of Tradition. By the Rev. Gerhard Pedersen, assistant to Professor Skydsgaard, Commission on Inter-Confessional Research, Lutheran World Federation 1960. m. (S Fr.1.50)

E. Flesseman van Leer: Einige Anmerkungen zu dem Artikel von Professor Leuba. (Prepared for the European Section, 1960.) m.

*S.L. Greenslade: Comment upon Leuba's paper "An Enquiry into Tradition based upon Systematic Theology". (Prepared for the European Section, 1960.) m.
**German translation*: Kommentar zu Professor Leubas Referat "Der Weg einer systematisch-theologischen Untersuchung über die Tradition." 1960. m.

J.J. Pelikan: Overcoming History by History. A "position-paper" presented as an Interim Report of the North American Section. 1960. m.

*K.E. Skydsgaard: Draft Interim Report of the Theological Commission on Tradition and Traditions. Presented to the Faith and Order Commission at St. Andrews, August 1960. m.

Study Commission on Institutionalism

J.L. Allen: Church Union and Minority Interests. (Revised draft of "Institutional Factors affecting Methodist Union in America.") SCI Paper no. 35A, prepared for the Commission, 1960. m.

*H. Dombois: The Church as Koinonia and as Institution. (Translated from the German.) SCI Paper no. 40, prepared for the Commission 1960. m.

*J. Gustafson and H. Wire: Actualizing a Church Union. (Revised draft.) SCI Paper no. 34 A, prepared for the Commission, 1960. m.

R.W. Lloyd: Union negotiations of 1937-1946 (Presbyterian Church USA and Protestant Episcopal Church). SCI Paper no. 37, prepared for the Commission, 1960. m.

*W.E. Mann: Institutional Factors in Canadian Church Union 1925. (Revised draft.) SCI Paper no. 11A, prepared for the Commission, 1960. m.

*W.D. Marsch: Der Begriff der Institution in soziologischer und theologischer Sicht der Gegenwart. SCI Paper no. 39, prepared for the Commission 1960. m.
English translation: The Concept of Institutionalism in the Light of Contemporary Sociology and Theology. m.

F.E. Rector: Baptist-Disciple Conversations Toward Unity. (Revised draft.) SCI Paper no. 26A, prepared for the Commission, 1960. m.

J.G. Winter: Union Negotiations of 1937-1946 (Presbyterian Church USA and Protestant Episcopal Church). SCI Paper no. 38, prepared for the Commission, 1960. m.